AGRICULTURAL SCIENCE
for the
CARIBBEAN

Ralph Persad

T0347614

OXFORD
UNIVERSITY PRESS

OXFORD
UNIVERSITY PRESS

Great Clarendon Street, Oxford, OX2 6DP, United Kingdom

Oxford University Press is a department of the University of Oxford.
It furthers the University's objective of excellence in research, scholarship,
and education by publishing worldwide. Oxford is a registered trade mark of
Oxford University Press in the UK and in certain other countries

First published by Thomas Nelson and Sons Ltd in 1994
This edition published by Oxford University Press in 2014

British Library Cataloguing in Publication Data
Data available

978-0-17-566394-1

30 29

Printed in Great Britain by Ashford Colour Press Ltd.

Acknowledgements

Illustrations: Ray Burrows, Corinne Clark and Andy Wright
Page make-up: Fox Design, Bramley, Surrey

The author and publishers are grateful to the following for permission to use photographs in
this book:
Barnaby's Picture Library: pages 73, 74.
Anne Bolt: pages 1 (top right, bottom left), 37, 58 (left), 121, 128.
Craig Burleigh: page 1 (bottom right)
Chaguaramas Agricultural Development: page 91 (centre left).
James Davis Worldwide Photographic Travel: page 3.
Robert Harding Picture Library: page 6, 9 (right), 123.
Robert Harding/Sue Ford: page 4 (left).
Holt Studios International/Nigel Cattlin: pages 59, 70.
Hutchison Picture Library/John Fuller: page 114.
Image Bank: page 125.
T Lacey MacDonald: pages 1 (top left), 4 (right), 9 (left), 57, 59, 90, 91, (top right, bottom left,
bottom right), 92 (bottom right).
David Simson: page 10 (bottom), 27.
The line illustrations of weeds on pages 122–3 are based on those originally published in
Common Weeds of the West Indies by C.D. Adams, L. Kasasian and J. Seevaye, published by the
University of the West Indies, 1968.

Although we have made every effort to trace and contact all copyright holders before publication this
has not been possible in all cases. If notified, the publisher will rectify any errors or omissions at the
earliest opportunity.

Links to third party websites are provided by Oxford in good faith and for information only. Oxford disclaims
any responsibility for the materials contained in any third party website referenced in this work.

Contents

Preface

Agricultural Science is an integral component of the curriculum of our primary, junior secondary, composite, senior comprehensive and many senior secondary schools. This three-book series for junior secondary and middle school classes in the Caribbean, has been prepared as an observational/activity-oriented course, and is intended to assist teachers in their agricultural programmes through the encouragement in the pupil of an enquiring and practical attitude toward the subject.

To make the best use of this series it is essential that the teacher should read and study the lessons well in advance so that he/she can prepare the necessary teaching aids and experiments, both of which are vital in the effective teaching of Agricultural Science.

Pupils should be encouraged to investigate and find out more about agriculture in their own localities, and to keep careful records of their findings.

Most of the chapters are designed for teachers to begin their lessons with observations, followed by discussions, inferences, and the application of these inferences in agricultural practices. Practical activity is an essential part of this exercise.

The school garden should be established. This should contain plants and features that can be used for reference and study purposes. Field trips and demonstrations all help to make the teaching programme more effective and stimulating.

Every attempt should be made to integrate the agricultural studies with those of the general science and social studies programmes, as well as any other allied subject in the school curriculum.

Though teachers should find the text adequate, they should feel free to adapt the lesson material to suit their own locality and interest, and to supplement the text with any further reading material that they may consider relevant and helpful.

R.S.P.
October 1993

1 What is agriculture?

Lesson objectives:

In this lesson we are going to learn more about agriculture. On completing the lesson you should:

1 have a general knowledge and understanding of the activities which take place in agriculture.

2 be able to state the importance of agriculture in the lives of people and to the country in which they live.

3 be able to identify some agricultural activities which take place in your village or community.

Here are some people working in **agriculture**. Study the pictures carefully and find out more about what they are doing.

Crop cultivation

Name the crops shown in the pictures on page 1.

Which of these crops are grown in your country?

Name three other crops grown in your home garden or school **farm**.

Crops are grown for many purposes. Bananas and yams are used as food, and sugar cane is manufactured into sugar. Forest trees help to protect the land and save water in the soil. A dairy **farmer** grows grass as a crop. How does he use the grass that he grows?

Livestock production

Name the animals shown in the pictures.

Which of them do you rear at home?

Which of them do you rear at school?

Why do farmers rear animals?

Animals supply us with food and clothing materials. From the cattle we get meat, milk and **hides**, and from the pig we get pork. Sheep give us meat for food and wool for clothing. Horses, mules, donkeys and oxen are used for work in the field or for carrying loads.

Some farmers rear bees and others rear fishes and prawns.

What agricultural products do these animals supply?

Manufacturing agricultural products

Name the manufactured products shown in the pictures.

What are the raw materials used in the **manufacture** of these products?

What advantages do manufactured products have over their raw materials?

Raw materials from plants and animals are processed into new products known as manufactured products.

These products can then be stored for future use or **exported** to other countries. Manufacturing helps a farmer to use up raw materials when they are plentiful or in excess of **market** requirements.

Here is an exercise for you to do.

Visit a nearby grocery and list the names of four agricultural products that are manufactured in (a) your country and (b) in a neighbouring or foreign country.

Marketing of agricultural products

Have you ever been to the market? Name some activities which take place there.

Observe the picture carefully and list the items that are on sale. Who grew or produced these items?

Farmers bring their crop and animal produce to the market. From the sales of these produce they get the money they need for managing their homes and operating their farms.

Experiments and research

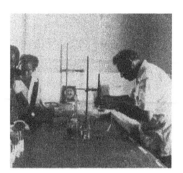

These pictures were taken at an agricultural research centre. Here research and experiments such as soil tests, variety trials, plant nutrition, pest and disease control and animal breeding are done. The information obtained from the research and experiments helps farmers to improve their farming methods in crop and livestock production.

Agriculture is a science as well as an art.

Now try to find answers for the following:

1 What is a variety trial?

2 What information is obtained from a variety trial?

3 How does that information help a farmer?

Summary

Agriculture deals mainly with crop and livestock production and the people who work in agriculture are called farmers. They cultivate crops and rear livestock which supply them with materials for food, clothing and shelter. Animals like horses, mules, donkeys and oxen are used for field work and for carrying loads.

Crops and animal products are taken to the market for sale. They are also used as raw materials in the manufacture of new products which could then be stored for future use or exported to other countries. From the sales of these goods farmers get money for managing their homes and operating their farms.

Research and experiments are important in agriculture. They give information on improved farming methods which help farmers to get better returns from the crops they grow and the livestock they rear.

Remember these

Agriculture	Activities dealing mainly with crop and livestock production.
Export	The sale of goods to other countries.
Farmers	People who work in agriculture.
Farm	An enterprise or unit in which agriculture is done.
Livestock	Animals that are reared by farmers.
Dairy animals	Animals reared mainly for milk production.
Hides	The preserved skins of animals.
Manufacture	The processing of raw materials to give a new product.
Market	A place where goods are bought and sold.
Research	The use of records or experiments to get new information.

Practical activities

Here are two practical activities for you to do.

1 Look around your home or school compound and collect **three** samples of food products obtained from (a) crops and (b) animals.

2 Visit a nearby animal farm or vegetable garden. Look at what is going on and make a note of the activities in your notebook.

Do these test exercises

1 Consider these statements carefully. State whether they are *true* or *false*.

a Farmers are people who work in agriculture.

b The cultivation of grass and forest trees is not agriculture.

c Bees are useful in agriculture.

d Farmers obtain money from the sale of farm produce.

e Manufactured products have no advantage over their raw materials.

2 Select the best answer from the choices given.

a Chocolate is manufactured from:

  A coconut

  B cocoa

  C coffee beans

  D citrus

b Which of these is not an animal product?

  A sugar

  B honey

  C cheese

  D wool

c The word export means:

  A buying goods from other countries

  B selling goods to other countries

  C finding markets for manufactured goods

  D storing manufactured goods for future use

3 Complete the statements below by filling the blank spaces with suitable words taken from this list:

information, manufactured, supply, improve, experiments, materials, export.

a Crops and animals .... raw .... which are .... into new products.

b Research and .... in agriculture give .... which helps to .... farming methods.

4 Complete the table below by giving six examples in each case of crop and animal products.

Crops Products	Animal Products
....	....
....	....
....	....
....	....
....	....
....	....

5 Describe the activities which take place in each of the following areas:

a around the seaside

b in a forested area

c on low lying flat lands

d on steep slopes or mountain side

2 Agriculture supplies our major needs

Man has several basic needs and requirements in life. He needs food for health, growth and energy; clothing to protect his body, and a house for shelter and security. He needs to be educated and trained in technical skills which will prepare him for an **occupation** or for employment. He should also be able to use his **leisure hours** profitably.

Can agriculture supply these basic requirements in life?

Basic needs and requirements in life

The need for food

Why do you eat food?

What are the chief sources of our foods?

What foods do our animals eat?

Some of our foods

You will remember that food is essential for health, growth and energy. Foods are obtained mainly from the crops we grow and the livestock we rear.

The pictures on page 6 show you some foods eaten by man and by animals.

Complete the table below by listing the sources from which these foods are obtained.

Foods from plants	Foods from animals

The need for clothing and shelter

We wear clothes to cover our bodies and keep us warm; and we need houses to protect us from the weather or from the dangers of harmful animals.

Study the pictures on this page carefully and find answers for the following.

List the names of some materials from which clothing and footwear are made.

Which are obtained from plants?

Which are obtained from animals?

Clothing materials may also be made from **artificial fibres**. These are fibres that are manufactured from chemicals. A good example of this is nylon.

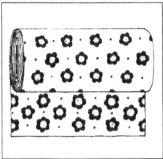

Raw materials for trade and industry

Agriculture supplies **raw materials** for trade and **industry**. For example milk is the raw material used in the manufacture of cheese, and cotton fibres in the manufacture of cotton cloth.

The pictures below show you some manufactured products.

What raw materials are needed for manufacturing the products in these pictures?
What does a firm do with its manufactured products?
What do we call the act of buying and selling manufactured goods?
What is foreign exchange?
Now complete this table in your notebook:

Local industry	Raw material	Manufactured Products
e.g. sugar cane	stem and juice of cane	sugar, molasses, rum, bagasse, celotex
citrus		
cotton		
cocoa		
coffee		
coconut		
dairy animals		
sheep		
pig		
forest trees		

Occupation and employment

Agriculture provides occupation and employment for many people.

People seek employment in order to support their homes and families. Some farmers are self employed; they own farms which are usually operated by the members of the family. Such farms are known as **family farms**. Owners of

large estates and plantations employ labour. On these estates there are several types of employment opportunities for people in agriculture.

What are the occupations of the people in the pictures on this page?

Now investigate and find answers for the following.
List six types of occupation found in agriculture.
Name four kinds of employment you can get on:
a a dairy farm
b a vegetable farm
c a sugar cane or banana plantation

Leisure time activities

The picture on page 10 shows a family at work during leisure hours. These are the hours when they are not at regular work but are engaged in a hobby or in some other useful exercise.

How are members of the the family using their leisure hours?
Name some agricultural activities which could occupy your leisure time, for example growing vegetables for the home.

List four ways in which leisure time activities in agriculture are valuable.

Income and revenue

A farmer depends upon an **income** to keep his home and his farming business going. In the same way a country depends upon an income (or **revenue**) to meet its **expenditures** and to pay for new projects.

A farmer obtains income from the sales of farm produce, and the taxes he pays go into the revenue of the country.

A farmer's income may vary from year to year. Why?

How can a farmer increase his income?

Can increases in farm production help a farmer and his country?

The better the crop, the better the farmer's income

Increases in farm production and improvement in the quality of farm products can bring in more income to a farmer and more foreign exchange to a country.

Summary

Agriculture supplies some of our basic requirements in life such as food, clothing and shelter. It also supplies raw materials for industry and trade.

Many people find employment in agriculture. Some people work on large estates and plantations while others operate their own farms. People from other walks of life also spend their leisure hours profitably in agriculture.

Agriculture is a major source of income to farmers and of revenue for the government. Farmers obtain their incomes from the sales of farm produce, and the foreign exchange obtained from the export of agricultural products adds to the revenue of the country.

Remember these

Artificial fibres	Fibres that are manufactured.
Expenditure	Money spent on running or managing an enterprise.
Family farm	A farm owned and operated by members of one family.
Income	Money obtained as wages from employment or from an occupation.
Industry	A business enterprise designed to produce a single product or a number of related products.
Leisure hours	The hours or spare time when a person is not engaged in regular work.
Occupation	An enterprise pursued as a livelihood.
Raw materials	Materials used in the manufacture of a new product.
Revenue	A source of government or business income.
Trade	The process of buying or selling or exchange of goods.

Practical activities

1 Visit a nearby grocery and look at the manufactured product on the shelves. Prepare a list of twelve products that are (a) derived from plants and (b) derived from animals.
2 Collect three samples of clothing material including footwear that are produced from each of the following (a) cotton, (b) wool and (c) artificial fibres.

Do these test exercises

1 Which of these statements are *true* and which are *false*?

a Foods are obtained mainly from the crops we grow and the animals we rear.

b Cheese is a manufactured product.

c Nylon is a fibre obtained from plants.

d The taxes we pay are a source of government revenue.

e Leisure hours are those hours spent in regular work.

2 Select the best answer from the choices given.

a Which of these is NOT considered a basic need in life:
A trade
B food
C shelter
D clothing

b Bagasse is a by-product of:
A cocoa
B coffee
C sugar cane
D citrus fruits

c Coconut is used as the raw material in the manufacture of all the following except:
A fibres
B textiles
C edible oils
D animal feeds

d The group of items representing manufactured products is:
A meat, milk, eggs
B wool, cotton fibres, hides
C citrus fruits, coffee beans, cocoa
D cheese, jams, jellies

e Foreign exchange is money obtained from the sales of:
A goods in the local market
B goods to other countries
C locally manufactured products
D raw materials to industry

3 Make a list of six food crops grown and used locally in your country.

4 What is a plantation crop? Name some crops grown in plantation in your country or in any other nearby country.

5 Give two examples each of clothing material which comes from (a) plants, (b) animals and (c) synthetic fibre.

6 State the benefits that can be gained by using ones leisure hours in the home garden.

7 A farmer is advised to increase the yields and improve the quality of his farm products. Explain the importance of this advice to the farmer and to his country.

3 The plant is the basic unit of agriculture

Lesson objectives

When you have completed this lesson you should be able to:

1 understand why plants are important in agriculture.

2 understand the process of photosynthesis.

3 describe how photosynthesis helps to maintain the balance of oxygen and carbon dioxide in the atmosphere.

4 explain how man, animals and plants depend upon each other for support.

In Chapter 1 we learnt that agriculture includes a number of activities.

Could there be any agriculture without plants?

How could people and animals obtain food without plants?

You will remember that agriculture deals mainly with crop and livestock production. Some of the crops that are grown supply food for man and for his livestock. They do this by manufacturing food substances which they store in their roots, stems, leaves and fruits. These foods may be eaten raw, cooked, or processed and stored for later use.

Look at the pictures on this page and make a list of some of the foods we get from plants.

Plants manufacture foods and raw materials

Nature's greatest factory lies within the leaves of plants. Here food and raw materials are manufactured. Man knows how this factory works, but he cannot artificially manufacture the same products as the plant.

Photosynthesis

Foods and raw materials are manufactured in the leaves of plants during the process of **photosynthesis**. This is a process in which certain substances are synthesized or put together to form other new substances. The diagram will help you understand this.

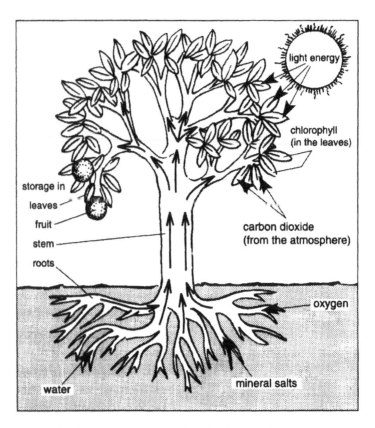

Mineral salts and water are absorbed from the soil by the roots and taken up through the stems into the leaves. From the atmosphere the leaves obtain **carbon dioxide** whilst the **chlorophyll** present in the leaves absorbs energy from the light.

The leaves take mineral substances, water and carbon dioxide and manufacture them into sugars, starches, proteins and oils. The process can only take place in the presence of light.

Some of the manufactured products are used by the plants for building their bodies whilst the excess is stored in the leaves, stems, fruits and roots. These are the raw materials that are of agricultural importance to man.

The balance of oxygen and carbon dioxide in the atmosphere

During the process of photosynthesis the leaves give off **oxygen**. This is the gas that humans and animals breathe in during **respiration**. When they exhale (breathe out) carbon dioxide is expelled into the atmosphere for use by plants. In this way the balance of oxygen and carbon dioxide in the **environment** is maintained. The diagram below will help you to understand this.

Balance of oxygen and carbon dioxide in the atmosphere

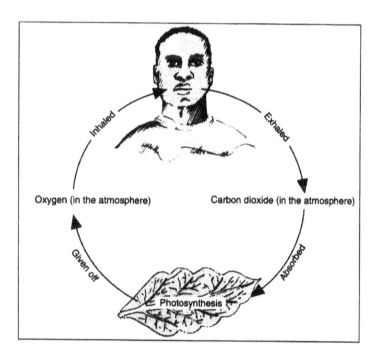

Inhaled

Exhaled

Oxygen (in the atmosphere)

Carbon dioxide (in the atmosphere)

Given off

Absorbed

Photosynthesis

Conditions necessary for efficiency in photosynthesis

Photosynthesis is one of the most important plant processes in crop production. This process takes place efficiently when crops get sufficient light, water and mineral supplies. The farmer ensures that these conditions are provided by removing shade and spacing plants properly to prevent overcrowding. Crops are **irrigated** and fertilised at periodic intervals so as to meet with their water and mineral requirements.

The importance of plants in agriculture

The figure below shows the importance of plants in agriculture. You will observe that the products from the crops we grow support animals, man and industry.

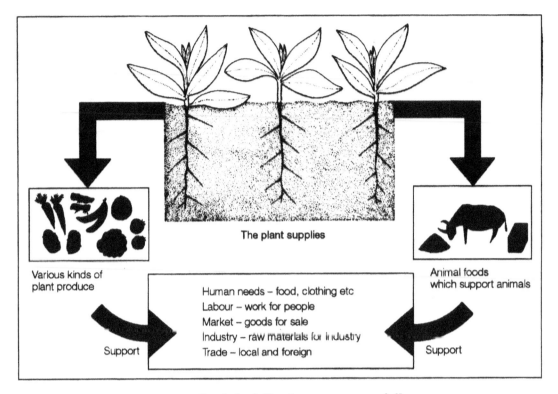

The plant supplies

Various kinds of plant produce

Animal foods which support animals

Human needs – food, clothing etc
Labour – work for people
Market – goods for sale
Industry – raw materials for industry
Trade – local and foreign

Support

Support

Read the following passage carefully.

"The farmer grows crops and rears animals. Crops supply foods for his animals and himself. Some crops, such as cotton and tobacco, supply raw materials for industry. Animals supply man with meat, milk and eggs which are essential foods in our diet. Their hides, wool and fur are needed in other industries.

When crops are grown on a **plantation** scale or animals reared in large numbers, the farmer may need labour and so he employs many other people to work on his farm.

Plant and animal produce are sold in the markets or as raw materials to the factories. Manufactured products are important items of local and **foreign trade**."

You should now make further investigations and find out how plants are supported by (a) man and (b) animals.

It is important for us to recognise that man, animals and plants depend upon each other for support. In other words, they are interdependent.

Summary

Plants are important in agriculture. They supply food for man and his livestock, and raw materials for industry. These substances are the products of photosynthesis, a special plant process which takes place in the chlorophyll of leaves in the presence of light. In this process plants take water, minerals and carbon dioxide and combine them to form sugars, starches, proteins and fats.

Since the process of photosynthesis is so important in crop production, farmers must ensure that their crops get adequate amounts of light, water and mineral supplies.

Photosynthesis helps to maintain the balance of oxygen and carbon dioxide in the atmosphere. As a result there is a constant supply of oxygen in the atmosphere.

The successful cultivation of crops on large estates and plantations requires a large work force. Here jobs and employment opportunities are provided for many people.

Finally we need to recognise that plants, animals and man depend upon each other. Without plants man and animals cannot survive, so it is essential for man to take great care of the crops and other useful plants in his environment.

Remember these

Atmosphere The gaseous substances surrounding the earth.

Carbon dioxide An atmospheric gas used by plants and given off by animals during respiration.

Chlorophyll The green colouring found in leaves and young stems.

Environment The objects or conditions which surround us.

Foreign trade Buying goods from or selling goods to other countries.

Irrigate To supply water to plants by means of channels, sprinklers or other devices.

Oxygen A gas used by plants and animals during respiration.

Photosynthesis A process in which plants take water, mineral substances, and carbon dioxide in the presence of chlorophyll and light and synthesise them to form sugars, starches and other food substances.

Plantation A large area of land cultivated with a single crop.

Respiration The process of breathing in plants and animals.

Practical activities

1 Visit your home or school garden and collect *two* samples in each case of food crops grown for the following parts:

a roots b stem c leaves d flowers e fruits

2 Make an outline of a variegated hibiscus or croton leaf and mark out the area on the leaf where photosynthesis is likely to take place.
State your reason for the area marked out.

Do these test exercises

1 Consider these statements carefully. State whether they are *true* or *false*.

a Chlorophyll is the green colouring matter found in the leaves of plants.

b Plants help to maintain the balance of oxygen and carbon dioxide supply in the atmosphere.

c Light is not essential in the process of photosynthesis.

d Irrigation is the process of removing excess water from the soil.

e Man, animals and plants depend upon each other for support.

2 Select the best answer from the choices given.

a Chlorophyll is found most abundantly in:
A the stems
B the leaves
C the flowers
D the roots

b Which of the following is *not* essential in the process of photosynthesis?
A light
B water
C oxygen
D carbon dioxide

c Irrigation is the process of supplying plants with adequate amounts of:
A light
B water
C mineral salts
D atmospheric gases

d Which group of crops is cultivated mainly on a vegetable farm?
A cocoa, coffee, citrus
B rice, corn, sugar cane
C banana, cotton, tobacco
D lettuce, tomato, carrots

e During respiration plants and animals:
(i) take in carbon dioxide and give off oxygen
(ii) take in oxygen and give off carbon dioxide
(iii) take in oxygen and give off nitrogen

In the statements above:
A only (i) is correct
B only (ii) is correct
C only (iii) is correct
D Neither (i), (ii) nor (iii) is correct.

3 Fill the blank spaces in the passage below with suitable words selected from this list:
oxygen, light, photosynthesis, sugars, water, respiration, starches, manufacture.

In the process of .... , leaves take mineral substances, ... and carbon dioxide and .... them into .... , ... , proteins and oils. The process can only take place in the presence of ....

4 Mention ten different types of occupation that agriculture provides for the people of your country, e.g. dairy stockman.

5 Here is a list of some foods that are imported into the Caribbean. Add ten more to this list.

salmon, onion, codfish, ... , ... , ... , ... , ... , ... , ... , ... , ... and ....

6 Draw up a table to show which manufactured products are associated with each crop from the following list.

sugar cane, coconut, tobacco, citrus, cocoa, sisal hemp, cotton, arrowroot, coffee, maize

7 Visit a nearby market or grocery and find the market prices of cabbage, tomatoes, carrots, lettuce, pumpkins, sweet peppers, plantains, sweet potatoes, cucumber and ochroes. These prices change from time to time. Explain why this is so.

4 The root system

External features of the plant

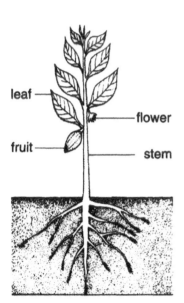

leaf

fruit

flower

stem

We recognise the plant as the basic unit of agriculture. Look carefully at any vegetable or orchard crop growing in your school garden and then say which of these statements about the plant is correct.

1 The whole plant lies underground.

2 The whole plant is above ground.

3 Part of the plant is above ground and part underground.

Now look at this diagram and fill in the blank spaces in the following sentences on with suitable words.

The plant is made up of _____ systems:

a the _____ system,

b the _____ system.

The **root system** lies _____. The **shoot system** lies _____. The shoot system is composed of the _____, the _____, the _____, the _____ and the _____.

The root system

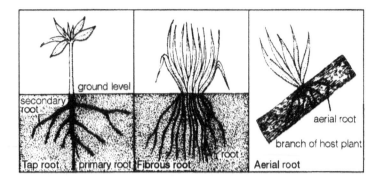

The pictures show you three types of root system. These are (a) **tap roots**, (b) **fibrous roots** and (c) **aerial roots**.

The tap root consists of a main or primary root growing downward into the ground. From the main root secondary roots develop and spread horizontally in the soil.

Fibrous rooted plants have no main or tap roots. Several roots of almost similar size grow from the base of the stem into the soil.

Aerial roots are usually found above ground. Vanden orchids and wild pines are good examples of plants with aerial roots.

The adventitious root

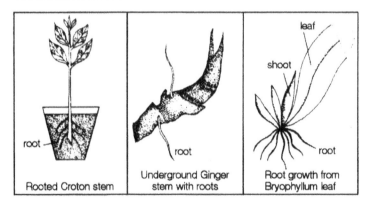

New roots normally develop from the root system of a plant, that is, they grow from older roots that are in the ground. However, it is possible to have roots developing from the stems and the leaves. These roots are called **adventitious roots** because they grow from part of the plant other than the **root system**.

The root tuber

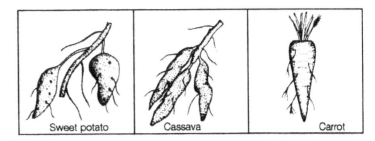

| Sweet potato | Cassava | Carrot |

The swollen roots of sweet potatoes, cassava, and carrots are called **root tubers**. They are modified roots which serve as storage organs. Some root tubers, like the sweet potato, cassava, eddoe, dasheen and topi-tambu, store large quantities of starch. These are known as starchy root tubers. Other root tubers like the radish, beet and carrot do not have a high starch content and are therefore said to be non-starchy.

Root structure and functions

All roots are generally similar in structure. The diagram below shows the external features that are typical of tap roots. Look at it carefully and note (a) the directions of growth of the primary and secondary roots, (b) the position of the root hairs on the root and (c) the anchor-like structure of the root.

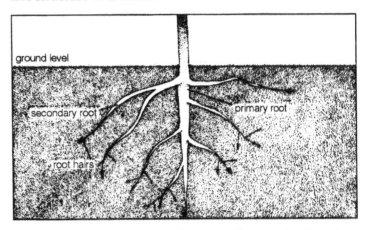

This diagram is an enlarged section of a root tip, showing the **root hairs**, the root cap (which is a protective layer) and

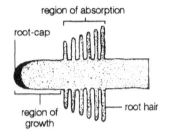

the region of growth. This is where root growth and development take place. You can also see the region of maturation which is now the developed part of the root.

Roots help to anchor the plant firmly in the ground. They absorb water and nutrient supplies from the soil by means of the root hairs. These substances help the plant to grow and develop.

Summary

The plant is made up of two systems. These are the root system and the shoot system. The root system generally lies underground. The shoot system grows above ground.

There are two main types of root: tap roots and fibrous roots. Tap rooted plants have a primary or main root with several secondary roots, whilst in fibrous rooted plants, the primary or main root is absent.

Roots (such as those of wild pines and orchids) may be described as aerial where they are above ground and exposed to the air; roots are called adventitious when they grow from other parts of the plants such as the leaves and the stem. When they act as storage organs like those of carrots and sweet potatoes, they are known as root tubers.

Root growth usually takes place at the tip of the roots. Here also are the root cap and the root hairs.

The main functions of the roots are to anchor the plant firmly in the ground and to absorb water and nutrients.

Remember these

Adventitious roots	Roots that grow and develop from those parts of the plant other than the root system.
Aerial roots	Roots that are exposed to air, light and rainfall.
Fibrous rooted plants	Plants without a primary root system. The roots are almost equal in size and grow in a bunch from the base of the stem.
Region of growth	The portion of root between the root cap and the root hairs where elongation or root growth takes place.
Root cap	A special protective tissue found at the root tip.
Root hairs	Hair-like structures found at the root tips.
Root system	The parts of the plant which develop underground.
Root tubers	Roots that are modified to act as storage organs.
Shoot system	The parts of the plant which grow above ground.
Tap rooted plants	Plants with a main or primary root from which secondary roots grow and develop.

Practical activities

1 Collect root systems of the following plants: pigeon peas, ochro, corn, tomato, sugar cane, carrot, sweet pepper, elephant grass, vander orchids, coffee, guava, wild pine, dasheen, radish and banana and group them in this table.

Tap rooted	Fibrous rooted	Aerial rooted

2 Germinate some bean or corn seeds between damp blotting paper in a dish. Look at the end of the root for the root cap, the region of elongation, and the root hairs. Draw a diagram of this section of the root and label it.

Do these test exercises

1 **Consider these statements carefully. State whether they are *true* or *false*.**

a The shoot system grows above ground.

b Roots grow and develop only from the root system of the plant.

c Secondary roots develop from primary roots.

d The tomato is a fibrous rooted plant.

e The carrot is a good example of a starchy root tuber.

2 **Select the best answer from the choices given.**

a Which group of plants is tap rooted?
A sugar cane, rice, corn
B sweet pepper, tomato, ochro
C dasheen, sweet potato, cassava
D vander orchids, wild pine, ginger

b The root development shown in the diagram is best described as :
A primary

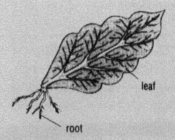

leaf

root

B secondary
C tuberous
D adventitious

c The function of the root hairs is to:
A protect the roots
B absorb water and nutrient supplies
C promote root growth
D anchor the plant in the ground

d Which of these is *not* a root tuber?
A eddoe
B radish
C cucumber
D carrot

e These statements refer to the carrot plant
(i) It is tap rooted.
(ii) The root acts as a storage organ.

(iii) The root anchors the plant firmly in the ground.
In the statements above:
A Only (i) is correct.
B Only (ii) is correct.
C Only (iii) is correct.
D (i), (ii) and (iii) are all correct.

3 **Study the tubers listed in the following table and indicate whether they are starchy or non-starchy.**

Root tubers	Starchy or non-starchy
e.g. sweet potato	starchy
carrot	....
cassava	....
radish	....
beet	....
topi-tambu	....

4 **Give two examples of plants with (a) tap roots, (b) fibrous roots and (c) aerial roots.**

5 **Make a list of the functions of the root.**

6 **In a windstorm the banana plants on an estate were uprooted, but the citrus were not. What reasons can you give for this?**

5 The shoot system

The shoot system

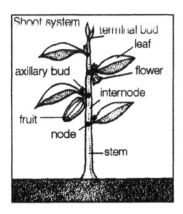

The shoot system forms the aerial part of the plant and consists of the stem, leaves, flowers and fruits. The diagram on the left shows you the structure of a typical shoot. Observe it carefully and locate the position of the **terminal bud**, the **axillary buds**, the **nodes** and **internodes**.

How does the growth of these two types of buds influence the growth pattern of the shoot?

Do the leaves and axillary buds grow at the nodes or internodes?

What parts of the shoot are supported by the stem?

Some types of shoot system

Many of our agricultural crops and ornamental plants have shoot systems like those in the pictures opposite.

From these pictures we can classify or group the shoot systems as follows.

Shoot system	Example of plant
Tree	mango
Shrub	croton
Grass	sugar cane
Creeper	black pepper
Twiner	yam
Runner	sweet potato

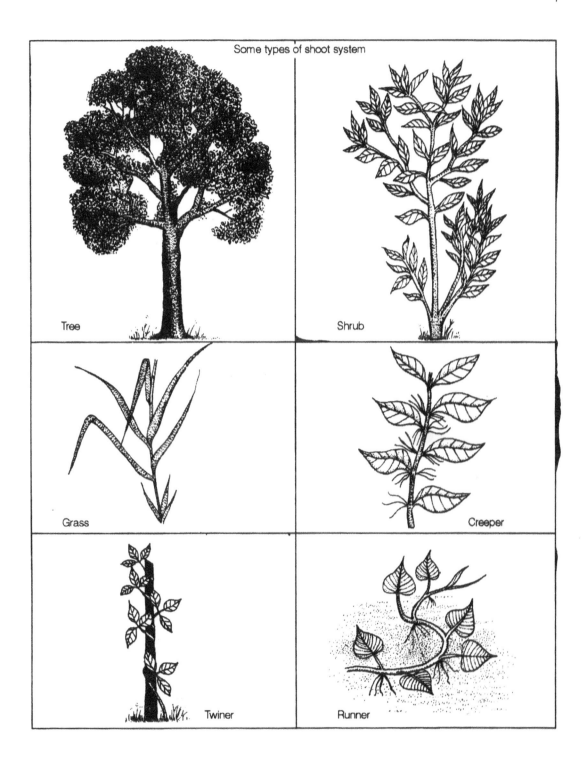

Some types of shoot system

Tree

Shrub

Grass

Creeper

Twiner

Runner

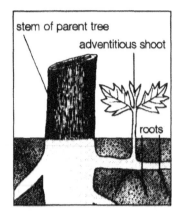

stem of parent tree
adventitious shoot
roots

Now give one additional example of a plant in each type of the shoot systems listed in the table.

The adventitious shoot

New shoots usually develop from axillary buds present on the stem and branches of the plant. However, shoots may also develop from the root system of the plant, giving rise to the **adventitious shoot**.

Adventitious shoots are quite common in plants like breadfruit, ixora, and casuarina. These shoots are often used in the propagation of new plants.

The stem

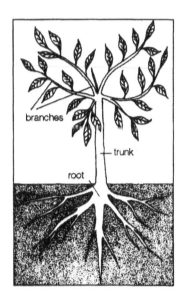

branches
trunk
root

Observe a citrus or mango tree carefully. You will notice that the main stem or trunk grows vertically, that is, upward in the air, whilst branches grow and spread horizontally. The stem and branches support the leaves, flowers and fruits and also serve as channels which take water and nutrients from the roots to the leaves.

Stems are classified as hard and woody or **herbaceous**, that is, soft. For example, mango and citrus plants have hard woody stems, while those of tomatoes and other vegetable crops are herbaceous.

Stems show other types of variation. They may be rounded or angular, solid or hollow, smooth or rough and prickly or jointed as in grasses. They may also show differences in colour.

The underground stem

The pictures on the left show you some types of underground stems. These stems are found in the ground. From them new roots and shoots grow. They are generally thick and swollen and act as storage organs. They are known as organs of perennation because they store food substances and give rise to new plants.

Some underground stems used as food are those of ginger, yam, dasheen, eddoe, tannia and arrowroot.

There is a simple classification of underground stems at the top of page 27.

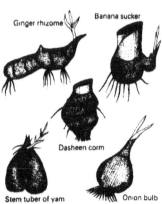

Ginger rhizome
Banana sucker
Dasheen corm
Stem tuber of yam
Onion bulb

A mango tree

Kind of underground stem	Example of plant
rhizome	ginger
corm	dasheen
sucker	banana
bulb	onion
stem tuber	yam

The leaves

Trees are covered with leaves. These leaves are generally thin, flat and green in colour. However, they show considerable variation in size and shape. Observe an orange or a mango branch with leaves.

How are the leaves connected to the branches?

What gives the leaves their green colour?

Why are the leaves thin and flat?

Parts of a leaf

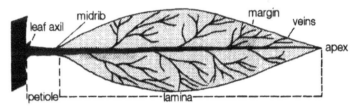

The picture above shows you the parts of a cocoa leaf. The midrib and veins serve as the framework for the flat surface of the lamina or leafblade. They are the channels through which water and mineral substances enter the leaves. Food substances manufactured by the leaves also pass through the midrib and veins to be transported to other parts of the plant. The apex is spear shaped whilst the leaf margin is smooth.

Variation in leaves

Leaves vary in shape. The diagrams below show you some of the differences.

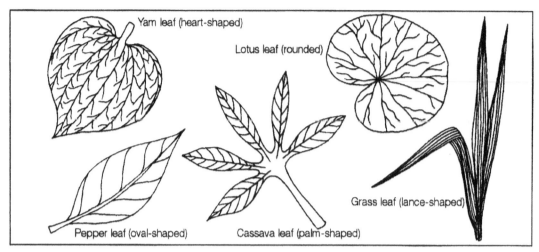

Types of leaf margin

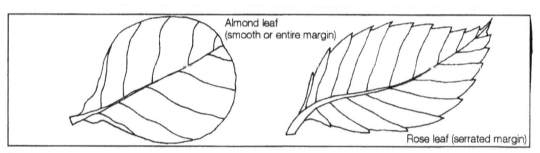

Types of leaf veins (venation)

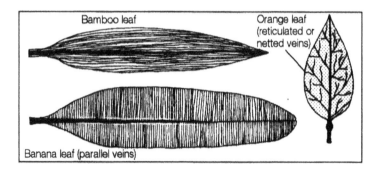

Types of leaf

Leaves may be classified as **simple** or **compound**. A simple leaf has a single lamina or leafblade as in the hibiscus or it may be lobed as in the cassava. A compound leaf is composed of two or more leafblades as in the pea plant or it may consist of several leaflets as in the cassia.

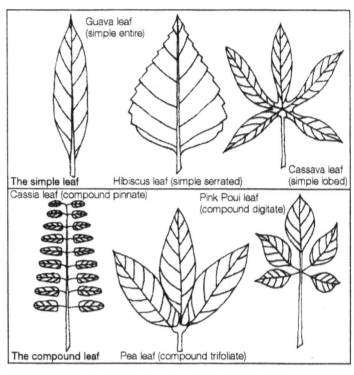

Guava leaf
(simple entire)

The simple leaf

Hibiscus leaf (simple serrated)

Cassava leaf
(simple lobed)

Cassia leaf (compound pinnate)

Pink Poui leaf
(compound digitate)

The compound leaf

Pea leaf (compound trifoliate)

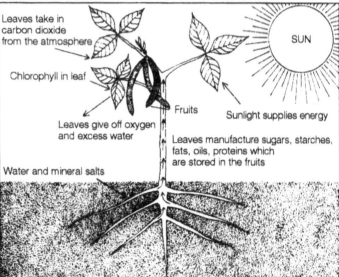

Leaves take in
carbon dioxide
from the atmosphere

SUN

Chlorophyll in leaf

Fruits

Sunlight supplies energy

Leaves give off oxygen
and excess water

Leaves manufacture sugars, starches,
fats, oils, proteins which
are stored in the fruits

Water and mineral salts

Under dark conditions leaves take in
oxygen from the atmosphere and give
off carbon dioxide.

How useful are the leaves to the red kidney plant? Study
the diagram carefully and you will observe that the leaves
perform three major functions. These are as follows.

1 Respiration – this is the breathing process in which
  leaves take oxygen from the atmosphere for use by the
  plant. Carbon dioxide is given off in return.

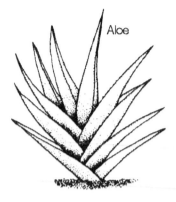

Aloe

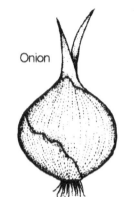

Onion

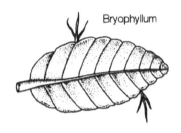

Bryophyllum

2 Photosynthesis – in this process leaves take in carbon dioxide from the atmosphere, along with water and mineral substances absorbed by the roots and combine them to form new substances such as sugars, proteins and fats. You will remember that this process can only take place in the presence of chlorophyll and light. Oxygen is released in return.

3 Transpiration – this is the process in which leaves give off water that is not required by the plant.

Other forms of leaf

Aloe

The leaves of the aloe are thick and fleshy. In these leaves the plant stores large quantities of water and food materials. As a result, the aloe can thrive under dry conditions and can survive droughts, whereas most other plants wilt and die.

The onion bulb

An onion bulb is made up of a set of inner and outer leaves. The inner leaves are thick and fleshy and act as storage organs. The outer **scale leaves** are thinner, and these protect the inner leaves.

The bryophyllum

The bryophyllum also has thick fleshy leaves which act as storage organs. In addition, there are tiny buds on the leaf margins. Can a new plant be propagated from a bryophyllum leaf? Why?

Summary

The shoot system is the aerial part of the plant and consists of the stem, leaves, flowers and fruits. Shoots vary in form and structure and are generally classified as trees, shrubs, grasses, creepers, twiners and runners. New shoots usually grow and develop from the terminal and axillary buds of the plant. However, if they develop from the root system and they are described as adventitious.

The stem and branches may be hard and woody or herbaceous (soft). They support leaves, flowers and fruits and serve as the channels through which nutrient and water supplies pass through the plant. Some stems grow and develop underground. These are known as organs of perennation.

Leaves develop at the nodes of the stem and branches. They are generally flat and green in colour. Some leaves are made up of single laminae or leafblades and described as simple. Those with two or more leafblades are called compound.

Leaves are essential to the plant. They perform the major functions of respiration, photosynthesis and transpiration. Sometimes leaves are modified to act as storage organs or they may be used for propagating new plants.

Remember these

Adventitious shoot	A shoot which develops from the root system.
Axillary bud	The bud at the leaf axil on the node of the stem.
Compound leaf	A leaf consisting of two or more laminae or leafblades.
Herbaceous plant	A plant with soft succulent stem and leaves.
Internode	The part of the stem between two nodes.
Node	A point on the stem where the leaf and the axillary bud develop.
Scale leaves	The thin outer protective leaves of a bulb or other underground stem.
Simple leaf	A leaf with a single lamina or leafblade.
Terminal bud	The bud at the tip of the shoot that gives rise to vertical growth.
Transpiration	The process in which leaves give off excess water.

Practical activities

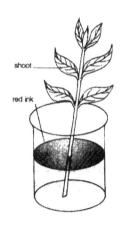

1 Try this experiment.
   Cut a shoot of a white balsam or a white periwinkle plant and allow the cut end to stand in a mixture of red ink for 24 hours. Now cut along the stem and state your observation. Relate this to the functions of the stem.
2 Collect stems of any *two* of the following plants: tomato, rose, cucumber, sugar cane, citrus. Observe them carefully and then answer these questions.
   Is the stem woody or soft? Is it rounded or angular? Is it hollow or solid? Is it hairy, smooth, rough or prickly? Is the stem jointed? What is the colour of the stem? Does it leave a scent on the hand? Could the bark of the stem be peeled off? Is the stem edible?
3 Collect a leaf from one of the following plants: coffee, orange, croton or pepper. Draw and label its parts.

4 Collect the leaf of an ochro and a croton plant and answer these questions after you have examined them. Is it a simple or compound leaf? Is the petiole long or short? Is the leaf green or coloured? Is it smooth, hairy or prickly? Is it dull or shiny? Is the leaf thick and fleshy? Does the leaf leave a smell on the finger after it is crushed?

5 Place the corm of an eddoe or a tannia plant in a container and cover with soil to a depth of 8 – 10 cm. Keep the soil damp by watering once every two days.
State your observations at the end of 3 – 4 weeks.

Do these test exercises

1 **Consider these statements carefully. State whether they are *true* or *false*.**

a Buds are found in the leaf axils of the shoot.

b Adventitious roots grow from the root system of the plant.

c Photosynthesis takes place in the absence of light.

d Leaves give off excess water.

e All leaves have long petioles.

f Some leaves are used for propagating new plants.

g Scale leaves are thick and fleshy.

2 **Select the best answer from the choices given.**

a Which group of plants is described as shrubs?
A mango, avocado, citrus
B ixora, hibiscus, roses
C sweet potato, cucumber, pumpkin
D cabbage, lettuce, patchoi

b Adventitious shoots are developed from:
A the terminal buds
B the axillary buds
C the root system
D the shoot system

c Transpiration is the process in which leaves:
A take in oxygen and give off carbon dioxide
B take in carbon dioxide and give off oxygen
C manufacture food substances
D give off excess water

d Scale leaves are found on all these root tubers except the:
A eddoe
B sweet potato
C tannia
D arrowroot

e The following statements refer to the leaf petiole.
(i) The petiole connects the leaf to the stem.
(ii) Food substances enter the leaf through the petiole.
(iii) The petioles of all leaves are short.
In the statements above
A (i) and (ii) are correct but (iii) is not.
B (i) and (iii) are correct but (ii) is not.
C (ii) and (iii) are correct but (i) is not.
D (i), (ii) and (iii) are all correct.

3 **List three functions performed by (a) the stem, (b) the leaf and (c) the midrib and leaf veins.**

4 **Give an explanation for each of the following.**

a The underground stem of the ginger is described as an "organ of perennation".

b The aloe thrives under dry conditions and can survive droughts.

c The lamina or leafblade is generally thin, flat and green in colour.

5 **Give *two* examples of each of the following.**

a Rhizomes: ....,
....

b Corms: ...., ...

c Bulbs: ...., ...

d Root tubers: ....,
....

e Stem tubers: ....,
....

6 **Name four plants in each of the following groups.**

a fruit trees

b ornamental trees

c plants with climbing stems

d plants which run on the ground

e grasses from which human foods are obtained.

6 Flowers, fruits and seeds

Lesson objectives

On completing the lesson you should be able to:

1 identify the parts of a flower and explain their functions.

2 identify plants with different types of flowers.

3 understand the processes of pollination and fertilisation.

4 explain the importance of fruits and seeds in agriculture.

5 give a simple classification of fruits.

In the last chapter we learnt about the stems and the leaves of plants. In this lesson we are going to look at the flower, the fruit and the seeds.

Shoots with flowers and fruits

Here are the pictures of some shoots with flowers and fruits on them. Flowers generally appear on the young shoots, but in some plants like the cocoa and the soursop they may also appear on the stem and branches. Flowers differ considerably. They vary in size, shape, colour and structure. Some are highly scented while others are not.

From the flowers fruits and seeds develop.

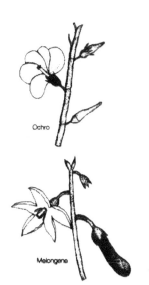

Ochro

Melongene

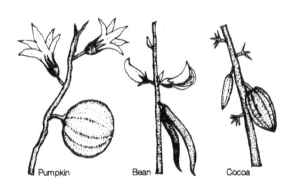

Pumpkin   Bean   Cocoa

Development of the flower

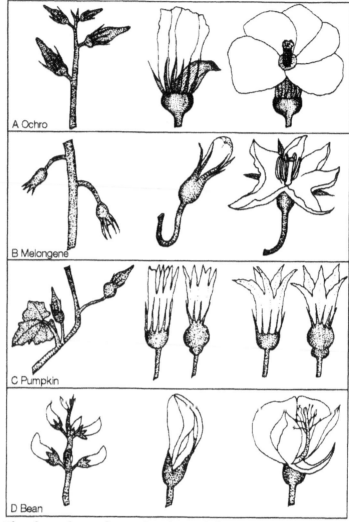

A Ochro

B Melongene

C Pumpkin

D Bean

The chart above shows the physical development of some flowers. Look at actual specimens and you will observe that some flowers appear singly on the stem. These are known as **solitary flowers**. Others appear in clusters commonly called an **inflorescence**. At first the flowers appear as tiny buds. These buds gradually develop into full bloom. What happens to flowers then?

Parts of a simple flower (Melongene)

Look at a melongene flower and compare it with the diagram on the next page. You will observe that the flower is made up of (a) the flower stalk or pedicel (b) the receptacle and (c) the major floral parts consisting of the sepals, the petals, the stamen and the carpels.

Let us look at the structure and functions of these parts.

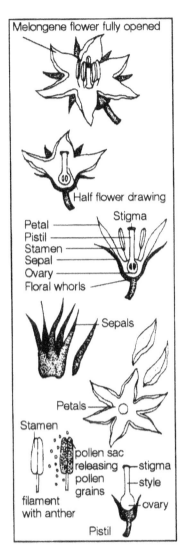

Melongene flower fully opened

Half flower drawing

Stigma
Petal
Pistil
Stamen
Sepal
Ovary
Floral whorls

Sepals

Petals

Stamen
pollen sac
releasing
pollen
grains
filament
with anther

stigma
style
ovary

Pistil

Pedicel (flower stalk)

The pedicel connects the flower to the shoot. It also serves as the channel through which water and minerals enter the flower.

Receptacle

The receptacle is the base of the flower which supports the major floral parts.

Sepals

The sepals are green leaf-like structures which enclose and protect the other floral parts while the flower is in its early stages of development. The sepals are fused, that is, joined together to form a cup called the calyx. In some flowers the sepals are free, that is, not fused. Examples of these are tomato and ochro.

Petals

There are usually five or six petals. These are fused and pinkish in colour. At the base of the petals are **nectaries**, which are glands that produce a sweet substance called nectar.

The coloured petals and the presence of nectar attract bees and other insects which help in the process of pollination.

Now look at an ochro or hibiscus flower and state (a) the colour of the petals and (b) whether the petals are fused or free.

Stamen

The stamen is the male reproductive organ of the flower. It consists of the filaments and the anthers which bear pollen grains.

Carpel (pistil)

The carpel or pistil is the female reproductive organ of the flower. It is made up of the stigma, the style and the ovary. The stigma is rough, hairy and sticky and accommodates the pollen grains. The ovary bears the ovules while the style connects the stigma and the ovary together.

Sex in flowers

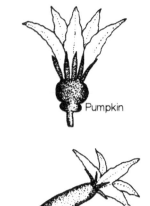

Pumpkin

Cucumber

We have learnt that the stamen and the carpel are the male and the female reproductive organs of the flower. A flower may be bisexual or unisexual. In a **bisexual flower** both stamen and carpel are present on the same flower as in the hibiscus.

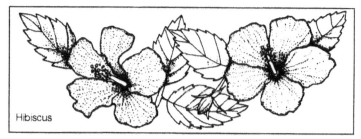

Hibiscus

In a **unisexual flower**, the male and the female parts are on separate flowers which may be on the same plant as in the pumpkin and cucumber, or on separate trees as in the pawpaw.

Pollination and fertilisation

stigma

pollen grains
pollen tube

ovules

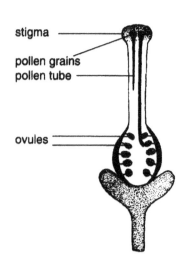

Pollen grains are released from the anthers. They are the male sex cells and are transferred to the stigma by natural agents such as insects, birds, water during rainfall and the wind. However, they may also be transferred artificially by man. The process of transferring pollen from the anthers to the stigma is called **pollination**. If the pollen comes from the same flower, the process is described as self-pollination. If it comes from another flower, it is described as cross-pollination.

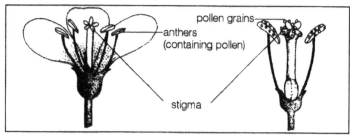

pollen grains
anthers
(containing pollen)

stigma

The diagram on the left shows you the germination of the pollen grains and the **fertilisation** of the ovules. The male sex cells travel through the pollen tube down the style to the ovary and fuse with the ovules, which are the female sex cells. The fusion of the pollen cells and the ovules results in fertilisation, a process which is essential for the development of seeds and fruits.

Is fertilisation important in agriculture? Why?

The fruit

Can you tell what fruit is being harvested?

Name six other fruits that are grown and harvested in your country, e.g. sapodilla, banana.

Development of fruit from flowers

Fruit and seeds develop from the female part of the flower, the carpel. After fertilisation, ovules develop into seeds and the ovary develops into the fruit which encases and protects the seeds.

Classification of fruit

Dry and juicy fruit

Some fruits are classified as dry and others as juicy. For example coconut, corn and pigeon peas are known as dry fruits. When they ripen they become dry and hard. They are not easily damaged and can be stored for a long time after harvesting.

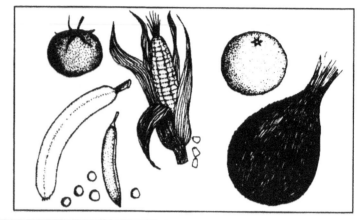

Fruits like oranges and tomatoes are described as juicy. When they ripen they become soft and they are filled with juice. These fruits are easily damaged and cannot be stored for long periods after harvesting.

Dehiscent and indehiscent fruit

Dehiscent fruits are those that split open when they are ripe. This is common in **legumes**, that is, plants belonging to the bean family. Other fruits like pawpaw and tomato are indehiscent. These do not split open when they are ripe.

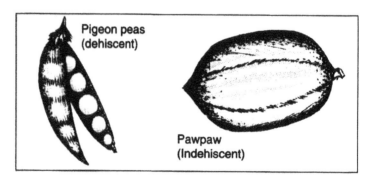

Pigeon peas
(dehiscent)

Pawpaw
(Indehiscent)

Other forms of fruit

Here are two other forms of fruit development. The cashew, which is popular for its nut, is described as a false fruit. The true fruit is the nut and the fleshy juicy part is the swollen receptacle.

The pineapple is an example of a **multiple fruit**. It is made up of a number of carpels fused together to give the thick juicy flesh that we use in our salads and fruit cocktails.

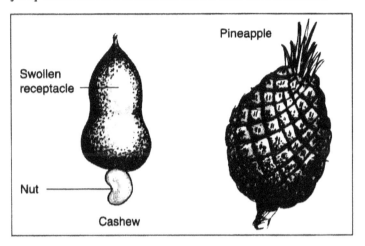

Farmers are interested in producing good quality fruits and seeds.

How are these important in agriculture?

Summary

Flowers generally appear on the young shoots of plants. They are found as solitary flowers or as an inflorescence. Flowers vary in size, shape, colour and structure. They may or may not be scented. From the flowers come the fruits.

A typical flower is made up of the flower stalk or pedicel, the receptacle the sepals, the petals, the stamen and the carpel. Each part performs a distinct functions but the two most important parts are the stamen and the carpel. The stamen produces pollen and the carpel contains the ovule.

A flower may be bisexual or unisexual. A bisexual flower has both stamen and carpel but in a unisexual flower, stamen and carpel appear separately.

Flowers produce fruit and seeds after they are pollinated and fertilised. Pollination is the transfer of pollen grains from the anthers to the stigma and this may be done naturally or artificially. After pollination there is a fusion of pollen cells and ovules resulting in fertilisation. The ovary then develops into fruit and the ovules into seeds.

Mature or ripened fruit may be classified as dry or juicy, dehiscent or indehiscent. If the fruit is derived from the fusion of a number of carpels it is classified as a multiple fruit and when it develops from the receptacle, it is considered a false fruit.

Fruit and seeds are important because they are used as food, for planting and raw materials for industry.

Remember these

Bisexual flower	A flower on which both stamen and carpel are present.
Dehiscent fruit	A fruit which splits open when it is ripe.
Fertilisation	Fusion of the pollen cells and the ovules which later develop into seeds encased by the fruit.
Inflorescence	A cluster of flowers on a single or main flower stalk.
Legumes	Plants belonging to the bean family.
Multiple fruit	The fusion of several carpels to form a single fruit.
Nectaries	Glands at the base of the petals which secrete nectar.
Pollination	The process of transferring pollen grains from the anthers to the stigma of the flower.
Solitary flowers	Flowers borne singly on the stem of a plant.
Unisexual flower	A flower which has either a stamen or a carpel.

Practical activities

1 Collect a hibiscus or an ochro flower. Observe it carefully and locate the sepals, the petals, the stamens and the carpels.

2 Take a walk through your home or school garden and collect *three* specimens of each of the following.
   a dry fruits
   b juicy fruits
   c dehiscent fruits

3 Collect specimens of seeds from twelve plants of agricultural importance. Comment on their size, shape, colour and feel.

4 Plant some corn, bean and tomato seeds in good moist ground. What do you see by the seventh day?

Do these test exercises

1 Consider these statements carefully. State whether they are *true* or *false*.

a Stamens and carpels are present on all flowers.

b Fusion of the pollen cells and the ovules results in fertilisation.

c Fertilisation is followed by pollination.

d The ochro has a bisexual flower.

e Dry fruits have a longer shelf life than juicy fruits.

2 Select the best answer from the choices given.

a The female reproductive organ in a flower is
A the stamen
B the petal
C the carpel
D the sepal

b The style in a flower
A supports the anthers
B bears the ovules
C connects the flower to the stem
D connects the stigma to the ovary

c Which of the following groups is classified as dry fruits?
A tomato, melongene, sweet pepper
B rice, soya bean, ochro
C banana, orange, pawpaw
D pumpkin, watermelon, cucumber

d An example of a dehiscent fruit is:
A pigeon peas
B banana
C corn
D pineapple

e Which of these is *not* considered a natural agent of pollination?
A bird
B insect
C man
D wind

3 Complete the following by filling the blank spaces with suitable words from this list:

stamen, man, ovary, ovules, water, stigma, fruit, style, petals.

Pollination is the transfer of pollen grains from the .... to the .... of the flowers. This is done either by means of the wind, ..., insects, or by .... himself.

The pollen grains germinate pollen tubes down the .... into the .... Soon the pollen cells fuse with the cells of the .... resulting in fertilisation. This is essential for the development of .... and seeds.

4 Give four examples of plants with (a) bisexual flowers and (b) unisexual flowers.

5 List six fruit in each of the following groups.

eaten as vegetables, e.g. tomato

used for making beverages, juices and jams, e.g. orange

used for canning, e.g. pineapple

6 Are the following fruit dry or juicy?

melongene, orange, coconut, mango, rice, sorrel, pigeon peas, pumpkin, guava, pawpaw, corn, cucumber.

7 What precautions should a farmer take in harvesting and preparing juicy fruit for market?

7 Our crop groups

Lesson objectives

At the end of the lesson you should be able to:

1 classify crops according to their uses.

2 name the basic food nutrients required by man and animals.

3 describe the functions of food nutrients in the body.

4 identify a range of food crops and state their food values.

Food groups

The pictures below show you some food crops placed in groups. Let us look closely at these food groups and try to find out more about their uses and their importance in agriculture.

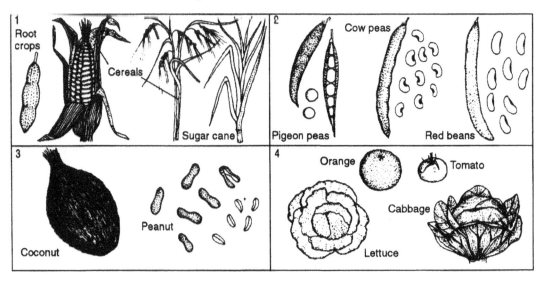

1 Root crops / Cereals / Sugar cane
2 Cow peas / Pigeon peas / Red beans
3 Coconut / Peanut
4 Orange / Tomato / Cabbage / Lettuce

Cereals

Name the three crops shown in this group.
Are these crops grown in your country?
How are they used by your people?
Cereals are grain crops produced by plants belonging to the grass family. They form the major source of our world's food supply. Cereals such as maize, rice and

sorghum are grown abundantly in the tropics, whereas wheat, oats, barley and rye are found mainly in subtropical and temperate countries.

Pulses

The illustrations show another group made up of beans. This group is called **pulses**. You will remember that peas and beans belong to the family of plants known as legumes.

Name the pulses in the picture.

State the ways in which these pulses are used.

Name some other crops belonging to the pulse group.

Fruit and nuts

Oranges, pineapples and pawpaw are soft and juicy. They are used for making crushes, slices and salads. The coconut is used as water nuts in the green state; when matured it is a rich source of fats and oils.

Vegetables

Name the vegetables in the picture.

Which of these are grown for (a) their leaves, (b) their fruits and (c) their roots?

What uses are made of these vegetables?

Classification of crop groups

From these examples we see that crops are grouped or classified according to their uses. The table below gives you a simple classification of our crop groups with examples of crops in each group and the purposes for which they are used.

Crop Group	Examples	Uses
Food Crops (a) Cereal	Maize, rice, sorghum, wheat, oats, barley, rye	Source of carbohydrate foods for man and animals.
(b) Pulses	Pigeon, peas, cow peas, red kidney bean, soya bean, lentil.	Good source of protein foods. Used as food by man and in the preparation of animal feeds.
(c) Starchy Root Crops	Yam, dasheen, eddoe, tannia, cassava, potato, arrowroot, topi-tambu	Rich in carbohydrates. Used as food for man and animals and in the manufacture of starch powder.

Crop Group	Examples	Uses
(d) Vegetables		Good source of vitamins and minerals. Used in the preparation of foods, salads and juices.
(i) Leafy Vegetable	Cabbage, lettuce, patchoi, mustard, spinach, callaloo bush	
(ii) Fruit Vegetables	Tomato, sweet pepper, melongene, squashes	
(iii) Root Vegetables	Carrots, radish, beet	
(e) Sugars	Sugar cane, beet	Source of carbohydrate. Used in the manufacture of sugar, molasses, and rum.
(f) Fats and Oils	Coconut, peanut, soya bean, maize, palm kernel, sunflower	Source of energy. Used in the preparation of oils, margarine, soap, animal feed
(g) Fruits and Nuts	Citrus, banana, pineapple, sapodilla, coconut, peanut, cashew nut	Source of vitamins and minerals. Used as fresh fruits and in the preparation of juices, slices, salads, jams and jellies. Coconut used mainly in the production of oils, fibres and animal feeds.
(h) Beverages	Coffee, cocoa, tea, mauby	Preparation of beverages cordials, powdered extracts
(i) Condiments and Spices	Onion, garlic, chive, celery, parsley, mint, basil, shadow benny, hot peppers, clove, ginger, tumeric, cinnamon, bayleaf, nutmeg, black pepper	Used for seasoning foods. Preparation of pickles and flavouring in drinks
Medicinal	Aloe vera, castor oil, peppermint, lemon grass, citronella	Used in the preparations of medicinal oils, rubs, creams, lotions and repellants
Fibres	Cotton, sisalhemp, coconut, jute	Preparation of threads, fabrics, ropes, mats, brooms, crocus bags, scrubbing brushes
Pasture-Forage	Pangola grass, paragrass, elephant grass, tanna grass, guatemala grass, lucuntu grass, pasture legumes, e.g. kudzu, centrosema, sirratro	Used as fodder materials for animals e.g. grazing grasses, silage grasses, preparation of silage
Forest	Cedar, mahogany, teak, mora, green heart, purple heart, wallaba, tirite, liannes	Used as timber for constructing bridges, lumber for house construction and furniture making, poles for piles and lamposts, materials for basketry.

Food value of crops

Many of our crops are grown for food. These food crops give us the necessary nutrients for good health, growth and energy. Our basic foods are carbohydrates, proteins, fats and oils, vitamins and minerals. These food elements perform the following major functions in our bodies.

Carbohydrates	Carbohydrates supply the body with heat and energy for work and play. They are sugars and starches.
Proteins	Proteins are essential for muscle development, body growth and for the repair of body tissues.
Fats and oils	Fats and oils also supply the body with energy. If taken in excess they are stored under the skin as body fat for future use.
Vitamins	Vitamins are essential for maintaining the body in good health.
Minerals	Minerals perform several functions, but they are most important in the formation of bones and teeth.

Study the food groups in the table given earlier in this lesson and then complete the circular chart below.

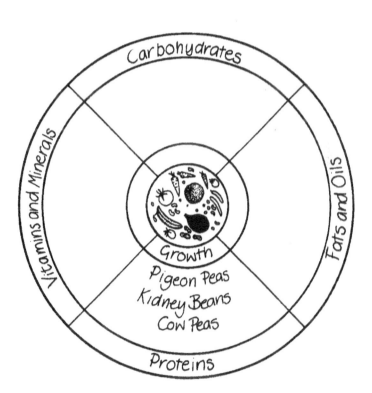

Summary

Crops are grouped or classified according to their uses. The major crop groups are food crops, medicinal, fibres, pasture-forage and forest crops. Among these groups, food crops consist of a wide range of plants which are further subdivided into groups known as cereals, pulses, starchy root crops, vegetables, sugars, fats and oils, fruits and nuts, **beverages**, condiments and spices.

Most of the people engaged in agriculture are involved in food crop production. From these crops we obtain our basic nutrients such as carbohydrates, proteins, fats and oils, vitamins and minerals. These food elements are essential for good health, growth and energy

Remember these

Beverage	A liquid preparation for drinking.
Cereals	Grain crops produced by plants belonging to the grass family.
Grazing grass	A pasture grass intended only for grazing by animals.
Pickles	Foods preserved in brine or vinegar.
Pulses	Edible seeds of leguminous plants.
Repellant	A substance which keeps off insects because of its offensive odour.
Silage	A product of grasses and other herbage materials which have been fermented and preserved in pits and silos as feed for animals.
Silage grasses	Grasses that are cut and fed to animals.

Practical activities

1 Collect three specimens of foods in each of the following groups.
   a cereals
   b pulses
   c starchy root crops
   d beverages
2 Collect samples of foods from the food crops listed below and classify them according to their food values.

   maize, sweet pepper, banana, spinach, beet, citrus, rice, eddoe, peanut, cow peas, pineapple, lettuce, soya-bean, sweet potato, coconut, carrot, squash, cassava and pigeon peas.

3 Obtain planting materials of six food crops used as condiments. Pot these plants and care for them until they are ready for use.

Your teacher will guide and assist you in this project.

Do these test exercises

1 Select the best answer from the choices given.

a Which of these food crops is a cereal?
A pigeon peas
B sweet potato
C rice
D carrot

b Which of the following is *not* a starchy root crop?
A tannia
B radish
C cassava
D eddoe

c The foods which represents the best source of fats and oils is:
A maize, coconut, soya bean
B cashew nut, peanut, pineapple
C carrot, arrowroot, sunflower
D peanut, sweet potato, beet

d Aloe vera is used in the:
A manufacture of oils and margarine
B production of silage materials
C preservation of pickled foods
D preparation of hand creams and lotions

e The body receives its supply of heat and energy mainly from foods that are rich in:
A vitamins
B minerals
C carbohydrates
D proteins

2 Name twelve crops that are grown for food.

3 List the basic nutrients obtained from the following foods.

Foods	Food nutrients
yams	carbohydrates
beans	....
rice	....
oranges	....
cassava	....
coconuts (dry)	....
patchoi	....
cabbage	....
bananas	....
beet	....

4 Complete the following sentences. The first is done for you.

a Carbohydrates give us energy to work and play

b Proteins
c Fats and oils
d Vitamins
e Minerals

5 Give two examples of crops used as:

a beverages
b condiments
c medicine
d fibres

6 Mother sends you to the market to buy foods for a luncheon meal. List some foods you will buy and say why.

7 Prepare a list of six forest crops and state the ways in which they are used.

8 Some countries are noted for certain crops or food products. Associate the following countries with some important crop or crops:

Jamaica, Grenada, St Vincent, Trinidad, Barbados, St Lucia, Cuba, Haiti, Antigua, Guyana, Venezuela, Belize and St Kitts.

8 Propagation of garden plants

Lesson objectives

At the end of the lesson you should be able to:

1 differentiate between sexual and asexual methods of plant propagation.

2 describe the parts of a seed and their functions.

3 identify monocotyledonous and dicotyledonous plants that are useful in agriculture.

4 understand the process of germination.

5 name the parts of plants used for vegetative propagation.

In this lesson you are going to learn about the propagation of garden plants, that is, the reproduction or multiplication of plants that are useful in agriculture.

Propagation by seeds

Mr Ram is planting his garden with corn and beans. What is his planting material? Is he using stem, leaves, seeds or roots?

Some plants such as corn, bean, tomato, ochro and cabbage are grown from seeds and these are said to be **sexually propagated**. You will remember that a seed develops from the fusion of the pollen cell and the ovule which are the male and female parts of the flower. However, plants may also be grown from other vegetative parts of the plant such as the root, stem or leaves, and these are said to be propagated asexually. Some examples of plants **asexually propagated** are bananas, tannia, ginger and cassava.

Parts of a bean seed

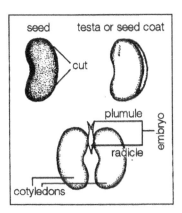

Soak a large bean seed in water for twelve to fifteen hours. Make a gentle longitudinal cut with a razor blade on the curved back of the seed and strip out the seed coat. You are now able to see the rest of the seed. Your teacher will help you to identify and label (a) the **testa** or seed coat, (b) the cotyledons or seed leaves and (c) the **embryo** which consists of the plumule and the radicle.

These parts have many uses in the life of the seed, as well as the plant which grows out of it. The table below tells you more about these parts and their functions.

Parts of the seed	Functions
Testa	Gives protection to the cotyledons and embryo in their early stages.
Cotyledon	Stores food materials for the young plant.
Embryo	Consists of the plumule and the radicle and gives rise to the new plant.
Plumule	Grows to become the shoot.
Radicle	Develops into the root system.

Parts of a corn seed

Collect some corn seeds and set them in a petri dish with damp blotting paper for three to five days. Now look at the soaked as well as the germinating corn seeds. You will observe that the testa is fused and there is only one cotyledon. There is an extra food storage organ called an endosperm. An embryo consisting of a plumule and a radicle is also present.

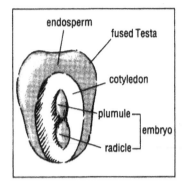

endosperm
fused Testa
cotyledon
plumule
embryo
radicle

Complete the following observations on non-germinated as well as germinated bean and corn seeds.

Observations	Bean	Corn
Is the testa free or fused?		
How many cotyledons are there?		
After germination, do the cotyledons remain below ground or do they come above ground?		
Is there an extra food storage organ, that is, the endosperm?		
Are the roots tap-rooted or fibrous rooted?		
Are the leaves narrow or broad?		

The bean is **dicotyledonous**; the corn is **monocotyledonous**. Can you say why? Use the observations above and find out six dicotyledonous and six monocotyledonous plants that are useful in agriculture.

Germination of seeds

What is **germination**?

Collect some pigeon peas or bean seeds from mature ripe pods and sow them in a box containing moist sand or damp garden soil.

Observe the seed for a period of six to seven days.

Did the seeds swell? Did the seeds burst? Did the seeds grow into seedlings? If they did then germination took place.

Germination can be described as the processes that a seed undergoes in order to grow into a seedling.

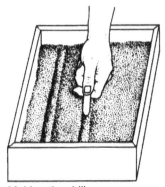

Making the drill

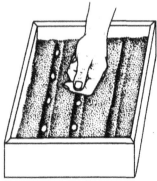

Sowing the seed

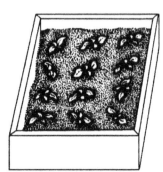

The young plants

Conditions necessary for germination

A seed is a living organism. It will germinate only if it contains an embryo that is alive. When placed in the soil, there must be an adequate supply of air, warmth and moisture.

In our practical exercises you will find out more about the conditions necessary for germination.

Propagation by vegetative parts of the plant

Earlier in this chapter you learnt that plants are propagated sexually by seeds and asexually by the vegetative parts of the plant. Let us look at some asexual methods of plant propagation.

Propagation by underground stems

Examine a ginger rhizome. You will notice the swollen stem which contains food materials and the presence of buds and roots. If the rhizome is placed in damp soil the buds grow into shoots and roots develop from the nodes. In this way a new ginger plant is obtained.

Think of three ways in which a rhizome is like a seed. Name two other plants that are propagated by rhizomes.

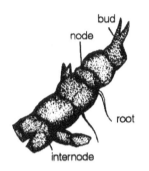

Bulbs

Now look at the onion bulb.

Does the onion bulb have a store of food material? If so where? Can the bulb grow roots? Can it grow a shoot? Does it give rise to a new plant? In what ways is the bulb like a rhizome?

Here are some other types of underground stem from which garden plants are propagated. Add more examples.

Tubers
a. Root tuber e.g. sweet potato   b. Stem tuber e.g. yam   Corms e.g. dasheen   Suckers e.g. banana

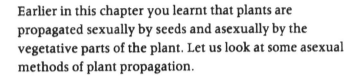

Propagation by cuttings

Plants may be propagated by stem, leaf or root **cuttings**. Examples are illustrated below. Add more examples.

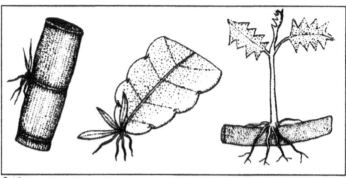

Cuttings
a. Stem cutting   b. Leaf cutting   c. Root cutting
e.g. sugar-cane   e.g. Bryophyllum   e.g. breadfruit

Propagation by separation

Chives are an example of a plant which can be propagated by **separation**. How many others can you find?

Propagation by bulbil

One example of this type of propagation is the yam. Which others can you think of?

Summary

Plants are propagated sexually by seeds or asexually by the vegetative parts of the plant (the stem, leaves and roots).

A seed consists of the testa, the cotyledons and the embryo which consists of the plumule and the radicle. A seed is a living organism. If given suitable conditions it will germinate and grow to become a new plant. The seed is the most common method of plant propagation.

Some plants do not produce seeds. These reproduce asexually by underground stems such as rhizomes, bulbs, tubers, corms and suckers. Others are propagated by cuttings, bulbils or by separation in the case of plants which grow in clusters.

It is important for you to know that vegetative parts of the plant are used for propagation because they contain a store of food materials and can produce roots and shoots.

Remember these

Asexual propagation	The use of stem, leaves or roots to propagate new plants.
Cuttings	Portions of stems, leaves and roots used in the propagation of plants.
Dicotyledonous plants	Plants grown from seeds containing two cotyledons.
Embryo	That part of the seed consisting of the plumule and the radicle.
Germination	The processes that a seed undergoes in growing into a seedling.
Monocotyledonous plants	Plants grown from seeds containing only one cotyledon.
Separation	The process of dividing a cluster of plants into single units for use as planting material.
Sexual propagation	The reproduction or propagation of plants by seeds.
Testa	The outer coat or covering of a seed.

Practical activities

1 Do all seeds grow?

Set the following types of pigeon pea seeds in a moist sand bed (25 seeds in each). Record the results.

Types of pigeon-pea seeds	No. of seeds set grown	No. of seeds
Green immature seeds		
Matured seeds (recently collected)		
Matured seeds (physically damaged)		
Matured seeds (damaged by insects)		
Very old seeds		

Which seeds gave the best germination results? Why?
Which seeds failed to grow? Why?
How many damaged seeds grew?
Why did some of the damaged seeds not grow?
Which group of seeds would you use as planting material? Why?

2 Get four containers, e.g. perforated plastic containers about 8–10 cm in height. Prepare and sow bean seeds, and treat as follows:

Jar no.	Preparation of jar	Observations after six days
No. 1	Place seeds in damp coconut bast or potting soil. Set to germinate in cool sheltered spot.	
No. 2	Set seeds in very dry coconut bast or potting soil. Set to germinate in cool sheltered spot.	
No. 3	Set seeds as in jar 1. Seal jar tightly and place in a cool sheltered spot to germinate.	
No. 4	Set seeds as in jar 1 and place in an ice-box or refrigerator to germinate.	

Which seeds showed good germination? Why?

Which seeds showed poor germination? Why?

Which seeds did not germinate at all? Why?

List three requirements that are essential for germination.

Give three reasons why a farmer should make germination tests before planting seeds.

3 a Collect underground stems of ginger, yam, eddoe and onion and set them in pots with damp soil to grow. Observe them for a period of three to four weeks and make the following observations.

(i) Did the buds grow into shoots?

(ii) Did root development take place?

b What was the source of food material for the plants during the early stages of growth?

4 Collect hibiscus or croton stems about the thickness of your finger. Cut them to a length of 25–30 cm and set them in potting bags to grow. Keep them in a shady spot and water regularly. Observe them for (a) shoot growth and (b) root development.

5 Separate a cluster of chives into single units and remove the leaves at a height of 16–20 cm from the base of the stem. Set them in potting bags with damp soil to grow. Make your observations at the end of four to six weeks.

Do these test exercises

1 Select the best answer from the choices given.

a A plant is sexually reproduced if it is propagated from:

A a stem cutting

B a corm

C a tuber

D a seed

b The part of the seed consisting of the plumule and the radicle is known as the:

A testa

B cotyledon

C embryo

D endosperm

c Which group represents monocotyledonous plants:

A coconut, rice, sorghum

B cucumber, watermelon, pumpkin

C tomato, melongene, sweet pepper

D ochro, pigeon pea, soya bean

d Suckers are used in the propagation of:

A ginger

B banana

C eddoe

D sweet potato

e In the process of germination:

(i) the plumule develops into the shoot

(ii) the radicle develops into the root

(iii) the testa provides food material for the new plant

Which of the above statements is true about germination?

A (i) and (iii)

B (ii) and (iii)

C (i) and (ii)

D (i), (ii) and (iii)

2 Make a list of ten plants that are propagated by seeds, e.g. ochro, pawpaw, ... , ... , ... , ... , ... , ... , ... and ....

3 a Draw and label the parts of a bean seed.

b Associate that part of the seed which performs the following functions:

e.g. Grows to become a plant. (embryo)

(i) Gives protection to cotyledons and embryo. ( )

(ii) Grows to become the root system. ( )

(iii) Stores food material. ( )

(iv) Grows to become the shoot system. ( )

4 Draw up a table to show whether the following plants are monocotyledonous or dicotyledonous:

cabbage, tomato, rice, melongene, sugar cane, corn, ochro, banana, pigeon-pea, sorghum, sorrel, onion.

5 a A farmer planted cabbage seeds and none grew. Give three probable reasons for this.

b Give three reasons why freshly collected bean seeds showed good germination in your garden plot.

c A farmer tested one hundred seeds. Eight-five of them germinated. Give two reasons why this test is helpful to him.

d give a good reason why corn seeds should be planted deeper in the dry season than in the wet season.

e Give one reason why bananas are not grown by seeds.

f List three ways in which a corm is like a seed.

6 Complete the following by using suitable words of your own.

a The vegetative part of a plant consists of the roots, ... , ... , and the ....

b The reproductive part of the plant consists of the .... , ... , and the ....

7 Name five plants that could be propagated by seeds as well as by other vegetative parts, e.g. onion.

(i) .... (ii) .... (iii) .... (iv) .... (v) ....

8 Complete the table below by indicating the chief method by which the following plants are propagated.

Plant	Chief method of propagation
Cassava	stem cutting
yam	....
sorrel	....
arrowroot	....
banana	....
sweet potato	....
rice	....
coconut	....
pumpkin	....
eddoe	....

9 Make drawings of the following underground stems: tuber, corm, bulb, rhizome, sucker, root tuber.

9 Cultivation of field crops

Lesson objectives

At the end of this lesson you should be able to:

1 outline the operations and practices involved in field crop production.

2 select seeds for use as propagating material.

3 cultivate one of the following crops: corn, bean, ochro, cucumber, lettuce

Field crop production

Many farmers are engaged in the cultivation of field crops such as corn, pigeon peas, cassava, cucumber, ochro, tomato, banana and several others including tree crops like citrus and mango. In producing these crops, a number of agricultural operations and practices are involved. These include the selection of planting material, land preparation, planting out, **irrigation**, weed control, insect, pest and disease control, fertiliser application and harvesting followed by proper care and treatment of the crop.

In this chapter you are going to study the cultivation of corn. You should then be able to cultivate other field crops on your own.

Cultivation of corn

Do you remember the crop group to which corn belongs? It is the cereal group. Think of three uses of corn.

Propagating or planting material
Corn is propagated from seeds. Can you say why? Only the best seeds should be planted. They should be uniform in size, well shaped, not physically damaged and free from insect attack. Why should we plant the best seeds?

Land preparation
Good land preparation is essential. The bushes must be cleared and the land tilled, drained and made into plots. Corn likes sunlight and grows best in a loose, aerated and well-drained soil.

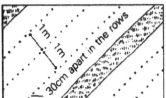

Planting and planting distances

Seeds are planted in rows 1 m apart and 30 cm apart in the rows. Only one seed is planted to a hole and not more than 1.5–2 cm deep.

Watering

Corn needs a lot of moisture to enable it to feed and grow well. In dry weather conditions, watering and irrigation are vital.

Weed control

Weeds rob plants of light, moisture and nutrient supplies. Weeds can be destroyed mechanically by weeding with cutlasses, hoes, or by spraying with chemicals called herbicides. Weeds should be destroyed in their early stages of growth.

These pictures show the difference that weeds can make.

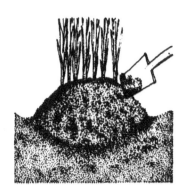

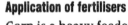

Moulding up

The plant is moulded up by the fourth to fifth week. This helps to remove water from the roots as well as to encourage the development of adventitious roots. These roots feed the plants and later on act as props.

Application of fertilisers

Corn is a heavy feeder and needs additional nutrient supplies in the form of fertilisers. Nitrogenous fertilisers like sulphate of ammonia are applied at the rate of 42 to 56 g per plant four to five weeks after planting, and once again at tasseling time.

Insect pest control

The chief insect pests which attack corn are the corn shoot worm, the corn ear worm and aphids. These pests are destroyed by spraying the plants with an insecticide. There are many insecticides in the garden shops; your teacher will give you the names of some of them.

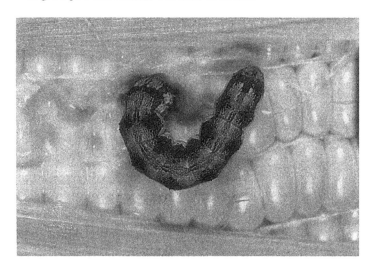

Maturity and harvest

Corn matures in three to four months. It is harvested as green corn or as dried corn. Green corn is eaten in soups, boiled or roasted. It is also canned as whole or crushed kernels. Dried ears are shelled and the grains are stored for home use or for future planting material.

Surplus grain is sold to be manufactured into cornflour or into poultry and animal feeds.

Summary

The production of field crops involves the following agricultural operations and practices.
1 Selection of propagating material
2 Land preparation
3 Planting out
4 Irrigation
5 Weed control
6 Insect pest and disease control
7 Fertiliser application
8 Harvesting
9 Care and treatment of harvested products
In the cultivation of corn, only the best seeds are used as propagating material. The land is cleared, tilled, drained and made into plots. The seeds are planted singly in rows 1 m apart and at a distance of 30 cm apart within the rows.

The plants are irrigated, moulded up, kept free from weeds, sprayed periodically to control insect attacks and treated with a fertiliser rich in nitrogen.

By the third or fourth month the crop is ready for harvesting. It can be used as green corn, or processed into cornflour or animal feed when it is dried.

Remember these

Aeration	Increasing the air content of the soil.
Drainage	The construction of drains to remove surplus water from the soil.
Fertilisers	Chemicals for improving soil fertility.
Field crop	A crop grown directly in the field.
Herbicides	Chemicals for destroying weeds.
Insecticides	Chemicals to destroy harmful insects.
Irrigation	Application of water to crops by means of sprinkler, channels, flooding, etc.
Moulding	The act of pulling soil around the roots of plants.
Tillage	Digging the land so as to loosen up the soil.
Tree crop	Trees cultivated for useful agricultural products, e.g. orchard trees such as citrus and mangoes or forest trees such as teak and cedar.

Practical activities

1 Collect seeds of corn, bean, ochro and cucumber from your school garden plot or from a nearby farmer. From the seeds collected (a) select a dozen seeds from each type for use as propagating material and (b) state the factors you considered in selecting the seeds.

2 Go to a garden shop and find out the names of three commercial types of fertilisers, insecticides and herbicides.

Chemicals	Examples of commercial types
Fertilisers	......................., ..., ...
Insecticides	......................., ..., ...
Herbicides	......................., ..., ...

3 On page 61 is a table on corn cultivation. Look at your garden plot to see how ochroes, beans, lettuces and cucumbers are cultivated. Then copy the table and complete it for these plants.

Crop	Propagation	Land preparation	Planting distances	Weed control	Application of fertilisers control	Pest and disease	Harvesttime	Uses	Say a little more
Corn	Seeds	Clear, till and drain	Rows 1 m apart. In rows 30cm apart	Weeding and use of herbicides	Sulphate of ammonia. 42–56 g per plant at 4–5 weeks after planting and at tasseling	Spray with insecticides against corn shoot worm and corn ear worm	Green corn 3–3½ months after planting, dry corn 4–4½ months after planting	Human foods, animal feeds, corn oil	Could be dried and stored for future use or as planting material

Do these test exercises

1 Select the best answer from the choices given.

a Corn is propagated by a:
  A tuber
  B corm
  C sucker
  D seed

b Herbicides are chemicals used for destroying:
  A weeds
  B insects
  C rodents
  D disease organisms

c Sulphate of ammonia is used in the production of corn as:
  A an insecticide
  B a weed killer
  C a fertiliser
  D a disease control measure

d The main reason for irrigating crops is to:
  A keep soil water in circulation
  B meet their water requirements
  C supply fertilisers through the water
  D destroy harmful soil organisms

e Weeds are controlled in their early stages of growth because it
  (i) reduces competition for soil nutrients
  (ii) is advisable to destroy them before flowering and seeding
  (iii) takes less chemicals and time to control them at that stage

Which of these statements about weed control are correct?
  A (i) and (ii) only
  B (i) and (iii) only
  C (ii) and (iii) only
  D (i), (ii) and (iii) are all correct

2 How is corn propagated?

3 Is this the only way of propagating corn? Why?

4 List the factors you will consider when selecting corn seeds as planting material.

5 Complete the sentences below to show that you know about land preparation for planting corn.

a Trees and bushes are cleared so that the plant can get plenty of ....

b Tillage helps to

c Drainage removes .... water and so helps to .... the soil.

6 Complete the following by selecting a suitable word or phrase from the brackets at the end of the sentences.

a When we irrigate a crop we apply .... (fertilisers, water, insecticides).

b Irrigation is needed in the .... season (wet, dry)

c Irrigation .... if corn is planted in the months of June or July. (is essential, may not be necessary)

d Corn is better grown on low-lying lands in the .... season (wet, dry)

e During the wet season it is better to plant corn on .... (the hillsides, low-lying lands.)

7 Complete the following sentences by adding suitable words of your own.

a Weeds rob plants of .... , ... and .... supplies.

b Weeds are destroyed mechanically by .... with .... and.............. or chemically by using ....

c Weeds should be destroyed in their early stages of growth because ....

8 Give good reasons why your corn crop should be: (a) moulded up; (b) fertilised; (c) sprayed with insecticides

9 List six ways in which green or dried corn could be used as foods.

10 Animals on the farm

Lesson objectives

Livestock farmers earn their livelihood by rearing
animals. This lesson introduces you to the main types of
animals reared on livestock farms. It also gives you some
general information about these animals. At the end of
the lesson you should be able to:

1 identify the major types of farm animals and the
  purposes for which they are reared.

2 classify farm animals according to size and external
  body features.

3 state the relationship between an animal's stomach
  and the type of feed it consumes.

4 identify the external body parts of a rabbit and a fowl.

Livestock production

Animal or livestock production is an important part of
agriculture. Many farmers are engaged in rearing animals
such as dairy cattle, goats, sheep, pigs and **poultry birds**.
These farmers earn their livelihood on the farm.

Here are some farm animals. Identify them by their
names and state the purposes for which they are reared.

Sheep Goose Horse Turkey Mule Pig Goat Duck Fowl Cow Water buffalo Donkey Rabbit

Complete the table below by naming animals reared for the purpose stated. An example is done for you.

Purposes	Animals
Meat and eggs	poultry birds – fowls, ducks, turkeys, geese
Meat and milk	
Mainly for meat	
Hair and hides	
Work/transport	

On some farms you may also find these animals. What useful purposes do they serve?

Some farmers live near large rivers or on the seaside. They find an occupation in fishing. Others construct ponds and rear freshwater fishes like the tilapia and the cascadura. At the present time farmers are also experimenting on the rearing of freshwater prawns.

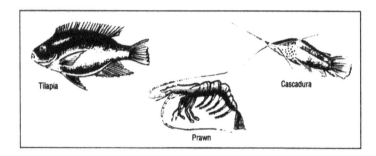

Name three other water animals that are used as food.

Classification of animals

Size of animals

The animals on a farm vary in size. Observe them carefully and name one animal that is (a) large, (b) medium sized and (c) small.

Use your observations to complete the table below by grouping the animals on a farm according to size.

Large animals	Medium sized animals	Small animals

External features

You have already observed that animals could be grouped according to size. However, they could also be classified according to certain common external features or characteristics.

Mammals

Mammals are warm-blooded animals. They are covered with hair and they breathe by means of lungs. They suckle or nurse their young ones and they use their limbs to move from place to place.

Name six farm animals that are mammals.

Birds

Observe the birds on a poultry farm, and then make a list of four types of birds reared by poultry farmers.

Birds like mammals are warm-blooded and they also breathe by lungs. They are covered with feathers and their forelimbs are modified into wings so that they can fly. They lay eggs from which their chicks or young ones are hatched.

Fish

Fishes are cold-blooded animals. They live in water and breathe by means of gills. They swim or move around by using their fins and tails. Some fish are covered with scales or with horny plates. Others are covered with skins. Like birds, fishes lay eggs from which their young ones are hatched.

Give an example of a fish that is covered with (a) scales (b) horny plates and (c) skin.

Body parts

The pictures below show you the external body parts of two small farm animals. Look at the live animals and try to locate these body parts.

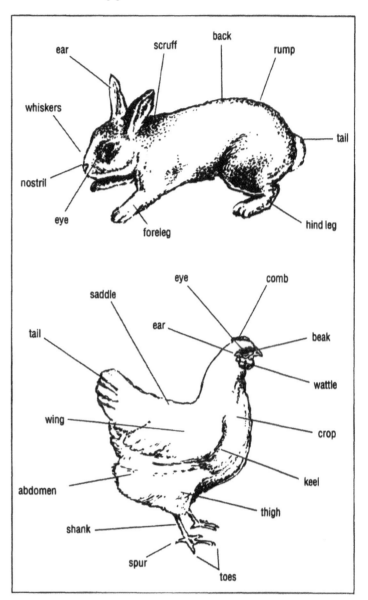

Farm animals and their feed

Farm animals feed on **succulent** herbs and fibrous grasses. They also feed on **concentrates** such as corn and soya bean meals. Pigs, rabbits and poultry birds have simple stomachs. They utilise concentrates and succulent plant materials. Goats, sheep and cattle can digest fibrous grasses because they have complex stomachs.

In a later book you will learn more about the stomachs of farm animals and the feeds they consume.

Summary

Livestock farmers rear animals such as cattle, sheep, goats, pigs, rabbits and poultry. From these animals they get meat, milk, eggs and hides. Animals like horses, mules and donkeys are used for work. Some farmers fish in seas and rivers or they may rear freshwater fish in ponds. Soon they will be rearing freshwater prawns as well.

Farm animals vary in size and characteristics. For example, cattle are large, goats are medium sized and poultry birds are small.

Farm animals are further classified as mammals, birds and fishes. Mammals and birds have two features in common. They are warm-blooded and they breathe by lungs. They differ in their covering and in their method of movement. Mammals suckle their young: birds do not.

Fish are cold-blooded. They live in water and breathe by gills. They may be covered with scales, horny plates or skin, and they use their fins and tails to swim.

Farm animals consume food to suit their stomachs. Birds and pigs have simple stomachs and they require succulent feeds and concentrates. Cows and goats have complex stomachs and they can digest grasses with high fibre content.

Remember these

Concentrates	Manufactured feeds with high nutrient value.
Dairy animals	Animals reared mainly for milk production.
Gills	The breathing organs of a fish.
Livestock production	Rearing animals as a form of agriculture.
Mammals	Warm-blooded animals that suckle their young.
Poultry birds	Birds reared for meat and eggs.
Succulent feeds	Soft herbaceous materials with high moisture content.

Practical activities

1 Go to a nearby fishing centre or market place and collect specimens of the following.
   a a fish covered with scales
   b a fish covered with horny plates
   c a fish covered with skin
   d a prawn

Place them in jars with a five per cent formaldehyde or alcohol solution. Label the specimens indicating their names, the date and the place where they were collected.

2 Visit a livestock farmer or a garden shop and collect a specimen of commercial feed (ration) for each of these animals: poultry birds, goat, pig, rabbit and cattle. Place them in jars or plastic bags and seal properly. Label the specimen.

3 Take a walk through your school farm and collect three samples of herbaceous materials suitable as rabbit feed. Label the samples and state the factors you considered in selecting them.

4 Make a drawing of a fowl or rabbit and label the body parts.

Do these test exercises

1 Consider these statements carefully. State whether they are *true* or *false*.

a All fishes are covered with scales.

b A dog on a farm serves as a watch as well as a pet.

c The cascadura and the tilapia are fresh water fishes.

d Poultry birds are reared mainly for eggs.

e Succulent feeds are high in moisture content.

2 Select the best answer from the choices given.

a Dairy animals are reared mainly for
A meat
B milk
C hides
D hair

b Which of these do *not* apply to mammals?
A They breathe by means of lungs.
B They are covered by hair.
C They are cold blooded animals.
D They suckle their young.

c Which group of animals is best suited for performing work?
A horse, goat, cattle
B horse, mule, donkey
C sheep, cattle, water buffalo
D cattle, goat, mule

d A cattle can digest fibrous grasses because it:
A is a large animal
B feeds on a variety of grasses
C chews its feed before swallowing
D has a complex stomach

e The following relate to fishes.
(i) They are cold blooded animals
(ii) They use their fins and tails to move
(iii) They breathe by means of lungs

Which of the statements above is true about fishes.
A (i) and (ii)
B (ii) and (iii)
C (i) and (iii)
D (i), (ii) and (iii)

3 Complete the following by filling the blanks with suitable words of your own.

a Birds are .... blooded animals. They are covered with .... and their fore limbs are modified into ....

b Sheep, ... and .... are mammals. They are covered with .... and they breathe by means of their .... They .... their young.

c Pigs and .... have .... stomachs. They feed on .... plant materials.

4 Give three examples of farm animals that are classified as (a) large, (b) medium sized and (c) small.

5 State two ways in which (a) birds and (b) fishes differ from mammals.

11 Poultry keeping

Lesson objectives

Livestock farmers engaged in poultry production rear fowls, ducks, geese and turkeys mainly for meat and eggs. In this lesson you are going to learn about some basic principles involved in poultry keeping. On completing the lesson, you should be able to:

1 state the purposes for which poultry birds are reared.

2 list three signs of health in birds.

3 describe three different systems of poultry management.

4 list the equipment that is required for rearing layer birds in a deep litter house.

5 select eggs for incubation.

6 describe the process of candling eggs.

7 describe the process of natural and artificial brooding of chicks.

8 give the names of suitable rations for baby chicks, broilers and layers.

9 name some common diseases and parasites of poultry birds.

10 list six methods of controlling diseases and parasites in poultry.

Poultry keeping

Abbie and Cynthia would like to be poultry farmers. They visit the poultry farm and watch the farmer at work. A good poultry farmer is a hard worker. He is also very careful. He ensures that his birds are well protected, well fed and free from disease.

White leghorns

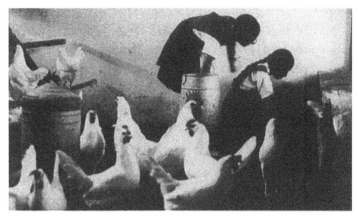

A healthy bird has a bright, alert look. It has a good appetite and its comb and wattles are always flush. It is active and uses its body parts freely.

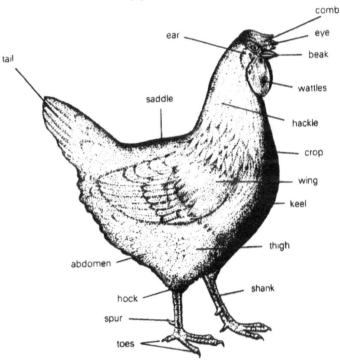

Now look at the birds again in the poultry farm and find out what uses are made of the following parts of the body.

The beak
For what purposes is the beak used?

Tails and wings
In what ways are the tail and wings useful to birds?

The feet

For what purposes do birds use their feet?

These body parts are essential. They enable the birds to feed, move and defend themselves.

The birds we rear

Birds are grouped according to the purposes for which they are reared.

Broiler or table birds

Broilers give us meat. They feed heavily, grow quickly and gain weight rapidly. Broilers are ready for slaughtering when they are eight to ten weeks old. By this time they should be about 2–2.5 kilograms in weight.

Layers or egg birds

Layers are reared for table eggs. They are light non-broody birds. A good layer lays as many as 200 to 220 eggs annually, that is, every year. The most popular laying birds in these areas are the leghorns and the golden comet.

Ducks are also good layers. However, they are scarcely ever used in the Caribbean for commercial egg production.

The dual-purpose bird

Some birds are reared for meat as well as for eggs, that is, they put on weight quickly and lay as many as 160 to 200 eggs annually. The Rhode Island Red, the Plymouth Rock and the New Hampshire Red are very good dual-purpose breeds. The Rhode Island Red is the most popular bird.

Rhode Island Red hens feeding

Breeders

Breeders are birds reared specially for fertile eggs. These eggs are incubated and hatched into chicks. Breeding birds are needed to maintain supplies of fertile eggs to the hatcheries, which in turn supply baby chicks to our poultry farms.

Common fowls

In households with small families the common fowl is reared. These are hardy kinds. They put on weight slowly, their egg production is low and they are generally **broody**. Common fowls are allowed to roam freely in search of feed which consists mainly of seeds, insects and succulent grasses.

Ducks, geese and turkeys

Ducks, geese and turkeys are generally reared as backyard birds to provide meat for the family table. Ducks, however, are becoming very popular and are now reared commercially by many farmers.

The turkey is a large bird. Its demand is greatest during festive seasons.

Systems of poultry management

Free range or extensive system

In the free range or extensive system birds are placed in an enclosed pasture to feed on their own. At night they are allowed to roost on trees or in a coop.

The battery cage or intensive system

In the intensive system a large number of birds are reared in a small area. Individual birds are placed in cages arranged in tiers that are in rows one upon the other and housed in a building. This system is costly to install, but it facilitates better care and management of birds than other systems.

Deep litter system (intensive system)

The deep litter system is the most popular system of poultry management in tropical countries. In this system the floor of the poultry house is covered with a layer of litter such as bagasse, wood shavings, sawdust or straw.

In this lesson the deep litter system of poultry management will be considered.

The care and management of birds

Spreading bagasse

Poultry house

We have seen that birds are reared for many purposes. No matter what the purpose, there are some general principles of care and management which apply to all types of birds.

Housing and equipment

In the Caribbean, poultry are generally reared in deep litter houses. Poultry houses should be located on high ground which is well drained. The building should be covered, ventilated, well lighted and free from draughts. The floor may be concrete or gravel. On this 8–10 cm of litter is placed. The litter absorbs moisture from the poultry droppings and helps to keep the floor dry.

The size of the poultry house depends upon the number of birds to be reared. Broilers need a floor area of approximately 30 square centimetres per bird, whilst layers and breeders need about one square metre per bird.

Poultry houses should be equipped with feed storage bins, water fountains, feed hoppers, perches and nest boxes. Artificial lighting is also desirable.

The selection and incubation of eggs

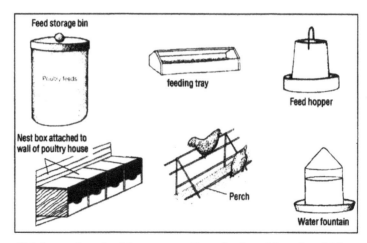

Feed storage bin

Poultry feeds

feeding tray

Feed hopper

Nest box attached to wall of poultry house

Perch

Water fountain

Chicks are hatched from eggs. Eggs for hatching should be selected from healthy birds in their first year of laying. Eggs should be fertile, clean, recently collected and of good size and shape. The shell should be firm and free from cracks.

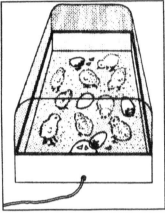

Eggs take three weeks (21 days) to incubate or develop into chicks. This is done naturally by placing the eggs under a broody mother hen or artificially in an **incubator**. An incubator must provide a few essential conditions for successful incubation:

1 A free circulation of fresh air.
2 A temperature range of 38.5°C–40°C during the incubation period.
3 Enough moisture to prevent the eggs from drying up.
4 A regular or automatic turning device in order to prevent the embryo from sticking to any part of the inside of the egg.

Candling of eggs

Eggs are candled at the eighth or ninth day. The eggs are examined by placing them against a ray of light. Eggs with developing embryo appear dark inside, whilst infertile eggs appear clear. In the **candling** process infertile eggs are removed from the incubator.

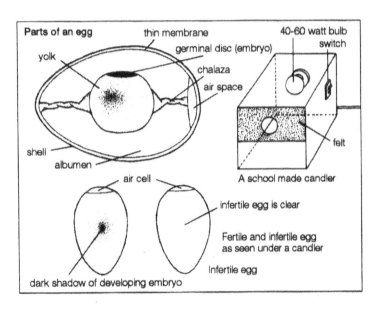

Parts of an egg — thin membrane, germinal disc (embryo), yolk, chalaza, air space, shell, albumen

40-60 watt bulb, switch, felt

A school made candler

air cell

infertile egg is clear

Fertile and infertile egg as seen under a candler

dark shadow of developing embryo

Infertile egg

Brooding chicks

Chicks need special care and attention in the early stages of growth. They may be brooded naturally or artificially.

In natural brooding, chicks are allowed to remain with a broody mother hen in an open run. The mother warms her chicks under her wings and takes care of them until

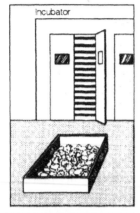

they are four to five weeks old. Chicks should be provided with adequate amounts of feed and plenty of clean fresh water.

Sanitation is very important. The run must be kept free from poultry droppings, whilst feed and water containers must be washed daily.

In artificial brooding, day-old chicks are kept in a brooder that is heated by kerosene lamps or infra-red electric bulbs. The initial temperature in the brooder should be 35°C, reduced by 2°C in each succeeding week until a temperature of 21°C is reached and maintained.

Feed and water should be provided freely, and must not in any way be contaminated with the droppings of the birds. A brooder with a wired floor and a dropping board would help to keep the birds off their droppings.

Whether the chicks are brooded naturally or artificially, they should be protected from **predators** such as rats and mongooses.

The feeding of birds

The poultry farmer makes sure that his birds are well fed. Give two good reasons why feeding is important.

Now make a list of feeds that you give to your birds.

Poultry rations

A good poultry feed contains the basic nutritional requirements of carbohydrates, fats, proteins, amino acids, vitamins and mineral salts such as calcium and phosphorus. Poultry rations must be complete and well balanced. They should suit the purpose for which the birds are reared, that is, for meat or for eggs.

Large poultry farms use manufactured feeds which are generally in pellet form. Poultry rations are of three types.

a Starter rations: these rations are fed to baby chicks up to the age of five or six weeks.

b Finisher rations: these rations are fed to broiler birds after the age of five to six weeks.

c Laying rations: these are fed to layers when they are twenty to twenty-two weeks old.

Requirements of baby chicks

Day-old baby chicks can stay without food for forty-eight hours after hatching. They continue to feed on the

remains of the yolk within them. However, they should be given a starter ration within a few hours of being hatched. Starter rations are rich in proteins and minerals. Can you say why? Finely ground chick grit and a good supply of fresh water should be provided. Chicks are fed 'ad lib' that is, their food troughs are always filled with feed, so that the birds can eat as much as they want.

The feeding of broiler birds

At the age of five to six weeks, broiler birds are put on a finisher ration. This ration is adequate in proteins and minerals, but its carbohydrate content is very high. At this stage, growth is rapid and the birds feed heavily and consume an abundance of water. Feeds must be provided plentifully and there must be a constant supply of fresh water.

The feeding of laying birds

Birds come into lay when they are about five to six months old. At this stage they are fed on a laying ration, which provides for their maintenance and the production of eggs.

Calcium is an important element in any laying ration. Can you say why? Do you know that the bones and the egg-shell are composed of calcium? Name some materials that are rich in calcium.

Like chicks and broilers, layers should also be fed 'ad lib' and be provided with a good supply of pure fresh water.

The control of diseases, parasites and pests in poultry

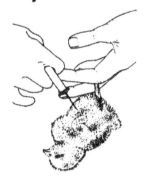

Farmer Ali is vaccinating his chicks. He uses a vaccine which helps to protect his chicks from diseases.

Farmers suffer great losses from diseases, **parasites** and pests. These often cause death, thriftlessness and a fall in egg production.

The table on the next page gives you information on some common diseases which affect poultry. Study them carefully.

Disease	Causative organism	Symptoms	How spread	Control
Marex	Virus	Paralysis, outstretched legs, one forward and one backward	Presence of the virus in the air and by contact	Destroy infected birds, practise good sanitation, vaccination
Fowl Pox	Virus	Lesions or blisters on comb wattle, eyelids, face and legs	Presence of the virus in the air and by contact	Vaccinate with fowl pox vaccine at 1 week old. Remove infected birds. Treat infected area with iodine
New Castle disease	Virus	Birds appear depressed; difficulty in breathing; twitching of head and neck; quick death	Transmitted through the secretions, saliva and droppings from infected birds	Vaccinate with New Castle vaccine. Proper sanitation
Coccidiosis	Coccidium in intestinal wall	Loss of appetite, bloody droppings, thriftlessness, finally death	Contaminated feed and water; by dogs, cats, mice and fleas	Use of sulphur drugs and medicated feed remove infected birds, avoid over crowding, good sanitation
Pullorum (Bacilliary White Diarrhoea)	Bacterium	Death of chicks first week after hatching; huddling of chicks; ruffled feathers; droopy heads, shrill chirping, loss of appetite, liquid faeces	Through the eggs; contaminated feed and water	Sanitation e.g. disinfection, use of foot bath, spraying of hatches, destroy carrier birds
Common Cold (Coryza)	Bacterium	Loss of appetite; coughing and sneezing, difficulty in breathing. Swollen heads, with cheese like substance	By contact with sick birds	Separate sick birds. Provide warmth. Use of antibiotic and medicated water and feed

Parasites

Internal parasites

The chief internal parasites attacking our birds are round worms and tape worms. They live in the intestinal tract and rob the birds of their nutrient supplies. These birds lose resistance, show poor health and their growth is retarded. In laying birds there is a drop in egg production.

Roundworms and tapeworms are controlled by **vermicides**. These chemicals are incorporated periodically into the feed and drinking water of the birds.

External parasites

What are external parasites? On what part of the bird are they found? They are found under the wings and feathers of the birds. The most common external parasites are lice, mites and ticks. These parasites cause irritation, restlessness and loss of energy. In laying birds, there is a fall in egg production. Birds infested with external parasites should be treated with a dusting powder such as sevin. Pens and poultry units should be sprayed with a disinfectant.

Other pests

Among the other pests attacking our poultry, rats and mongooses are the most prevalent. They invade stored feeds, suck eggs and destroy baby chicks. These pests are controlled by keeping the surroundings clear of bushes and rubbish. Traps and poisoned baits are also useful.

Remember these points about poultry keeping

1 Buy good, healthy chicks and vaccinate them against New Castle, fowl pox and bronchial diseases.
2 Debeak chicks when they are a week old. This prevents **cannibalism**, that is, chicks eating each other.
3 Ensure a constant and adequate supply of feeds and pure fresh water.
4 Feed birds the right type of rations.
5 Deworm birds periodically.
6 Avoid overcrowding in poultry houses.
7 Clean and disinfect poultry houses before introducing new chicks.
8 Keep visitors off the poultry farm. They may enter only after dipping their shoes in a foot bath.
9 Bury or burn all dead birds.
10 Good poultry keeping is a result of good sanitation and management exercises.

Summary

A poultry farmer rears birds mainly for meat and eggs. Fowls, ducks, geese and turkeys are commonly reared.

Poultry birds are generally reared extensively in the free range system or intensively in battery cages and deep litter houses. In the Caribbean and most tropical countries the deep litter system is preferred.

A poultry house should be covered, well ventilated and lighted, and free from draughts. The floor should be covered with litter. The house should also be equipped with feed hoppers, water fountains, nest boxes and perches.

Eggs for hatching should be fertile, clean, recently collected and of good size and shape. The shell should be firm and free from cracks. Eggs are incubated naturally under a broody hen or artificially in an incubator. The incubation period for chickens' eggs is 21 days and for ducks 28 days.

Baby chicks are brooded naturally by the mother hen or artificially in a brooder. The chicks are vaccinated, debeaked and provided with warmth. A supply of feed and fresh drinking water should be available. A high level of sanitation should always be maintained.

The rations for poultry birds vary according to the age of the bird and the purposes for which they are reared. Baby chicks and growing birds are fed on starter rations high in protein and minerals. Broilers in the final stages require a finisher ration with a high level of carbohydrate and layers on laying ration which takes care of egg production and maintenance of the laying bird.

Birds are usually fed 'ad lib' that is, there should be a constant supply of feed in their feed hoppers and troughs.

A healthy bird has a bright, alert appearance and a good appetite. However, birds may suffer from virus and bacterial diseases and from parasite infestations. These often cause death, unthriftiness or falls in egg production. In order to avoid these problems, a poultry farmer should stock his farm with good healthy chicks, have them vaccinated and provided with feed and adequate supplies of fresh water.

A high standard of sanitation and management should be maintained at all times.

Remember these

'ad lib'	To supply or provide feed without limitation.
Broilers	Birds reared for meat.
Broodiness	The tendency of a hen to sit on a clutch of eggs.
Candling	The process of detecting and removing infertile eggs set in an incubator.
Cannibalism	The act of a bird pecking at another's body parts.
Incubator	A piece of equipment designed for hatching eggs.
Layers	Birds reared for eggs.
Parasite	An organism which lives on and obtains its nutrition from the host.

Predators Animals which feed or prey on other animals.

Vermicides Chemicals used for destroying worms.

Practical activities

1 The eggs at your disposal were recently collected and are fertile. From the eggs provided:

a select six eggs for incubation

b state the factors you considered in selecting the eggs

2 From your home or school poultry farm, select 12 eight week old broiler-birds made up as follows:

4 large birds, 4 medium sized birds and 4 small birds

Find the average weight of the birds.

Use the calculation below to find the answer.

$$\frac{\text{Total weight of the birds}}{12} = \text{Kg}$$

3 Collect eggs from a batch of layers from your school or home poultry farm over a seven day period. Record daily:

a the number of layers in the pen

b the number of eggs collected

c the number of eggs cracked or broken

d the number of good eggs collected

Calculate:

(i)   The average number of good eggs collected daily. Do this as follows.

$$\frac{\text{The total number of good eggs collected over the 7 days}}{7}$$

Average number of eggs collected daily = ... eggs

(ii)   The average number of eggs laid per bird over the 7 day period. Do this as follows:

$$\frac{\text{Total number of eggs collected over the 7 day period}}{\text{the number of birds in the pen}}$$

Average number of eggs laid per bird = ...eggs

4 Visit a nearby hatchery and get the following information on the incubation of a batch of eggs.

a How was the incubator prepared for incubation?

b Take records of:

 (i) the date when eggs were set for incubation

 (ii) the number of eggs set

 (iii) the average temperature in the incubator during incubation

 (iv) the average humidity of the incubator during incubation

 (v) the date eggs were candled

 (vi) the number of eggs removed at candling time

 (vii) date of first appearance of chick's beak from shell

 (viii) date when most chicks were hatched out

 (ix) any other activity connected with incubation

 (x) the length of the incubation period

Do these text exercises

1 Complete the following by underlining the correct word or phrase in the brackets at the end of the sentence.

a Broilers are reared for (meat, eggs, meat and eggs).

b Birds reared for both meat and eggs are called (layers, breeders, dual-purpose).

c A good layer should be (broody, non-broody).

d New Castle disease is caused by a (bacterium, virus, coccidium).

e A vermicide destroys (bacteria, rats, worms).

2 Select the best answer from the choices given.

a The incubation period of a hen's egg is:

A 18 days
B 21 days
C 28 days
D 31 days

b Eggs are incubated at a temperature range of:

A 30.5°C to 31.5°C
B 32.5°C to 35.5°C
C 38.5°C to 40.5°C
D 42.5°C to 43.5°C

c A broiler house 6 m long and 3 m wide should accommodate:

A 150 birds
B 200 birds
C 250 birds
D 300 birds

d A batch of two week old baby chicks showed blood in their droppings. From this the farmer knew that the chicks were suffering from:

A Coryza
B Coccidiosis
C New Castle Disease
D Pullorum Disease

e Eggs collected from a poultry pen had thin shells with cracks. This indicated that the ration was deficient in:

A carbohydrates
B protein
C vitamins
D minerals

3 a State four methods of controlling poultry diseases.

b List three signs of a healthy bird.

4 What five points must be kept in mind when selecting eggs for hatching?

5 Give reasons for the following.

a Day-old baby chicks could live without food for forty-eight hours.

b Calcium is important in a laying ration.

c Carrier birds should be destroyed.

d Poultry houses should be disinfected before introducing new birds into them.

e Dipping your shoes in a foot-bath before entering a poultry farm.

6 Chickens are fed 'ad lib'. What does this mean? Why should chickens be fed 'ad lib'?

7 How are the following pests and diseases controlled in poultry?

a tape worms
b attack from rats
c lice and ticks
d pullorum disease
e fowl pox

8 Write a short paragraph saying how and why eggs are candled.

12 Agriculture is a business

Lesson objectives

In this lesson we are going to learn about agriculture as a business. On completing the lesson you should be able to:

1 identify or give the names of business enterprises in your village or community.

2 describe the structure of an agricultural business.

3 determine when a business is operating successfully.

What is a business?

Many people are engaged in business as an occupation. In your village or community you may see business enterprises such as groceries, hardware stores, fabric shops, animal farms, vegetable farms, citrus orchards, apiaries, lumber yards and many others.

Do you know why each of these enterprises is called a business? Examine them carefully by considering the following questions.

Is money invested in the form of land, buildings, equipment and stock?

Are people employed in the enterprise?

Is the enterprise subject to profit and loss?

If you get the answers "yes" to every question, then the enterprise examined is a business.

The structure of a grocery business

Study the diagram on page 82, showing the grocery as a business. You will observe that the **inputs** or **resources** are the building to house the grocery, the labour supplied by the grocery attendants, the stock or goods that are for sale and the management of the grocery by a manager. The **outputs** are the goods sold, and the monies made from these sales are the **income** or **returns**.

When the **expenditure**, that is, the money spent on the inputs is *less than the income* the business makes a **profit**.

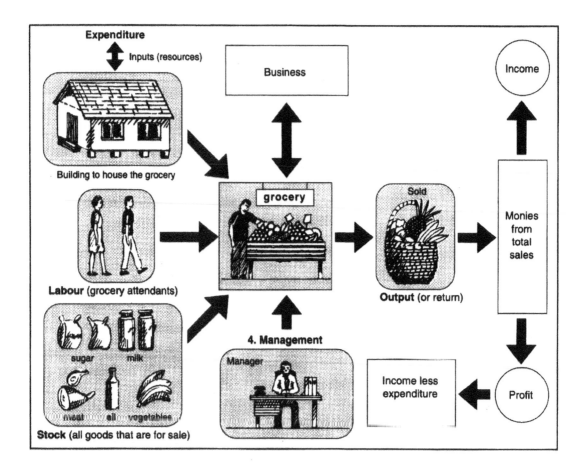

Farming is a business

The business structure of a mixed farm, that is, a farm on which crops are grown and livestock are reared, is shown on page 83. A good farmer operates his farm as a business. What are the resources of this farm?

What are the sources of the farmer's income?

How does a farmer determine whether his farm is successful or not?

Carefully study the inputs or resources on this mixed farm.

Make a list of the tools and equipment that are needed on the farm.

List all the work that a tractor can do on the farm.

What useful purposes does a spray can serve on a farm?

Give a single name for chemicals that are used for destroying (a) insects (b) fungi (c) weeds.

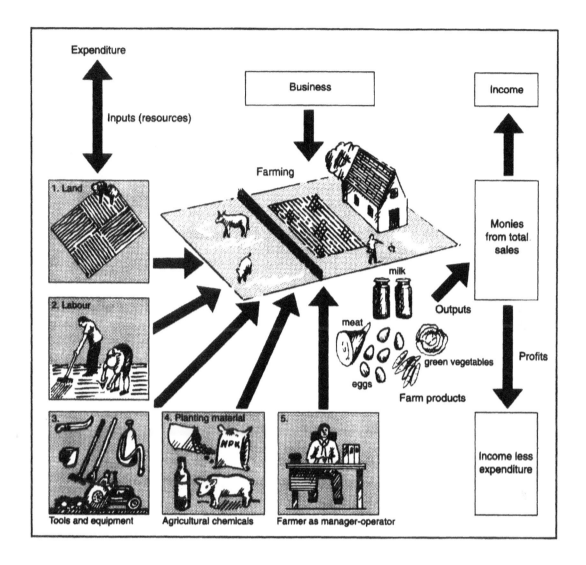

The business structure of a vegetable farm

The diagram on page 84 shows you the structure of a specialised vegetable farm. Study it carefully and then complete the table below.

Type of farm	Items of expenditure	Sources of income

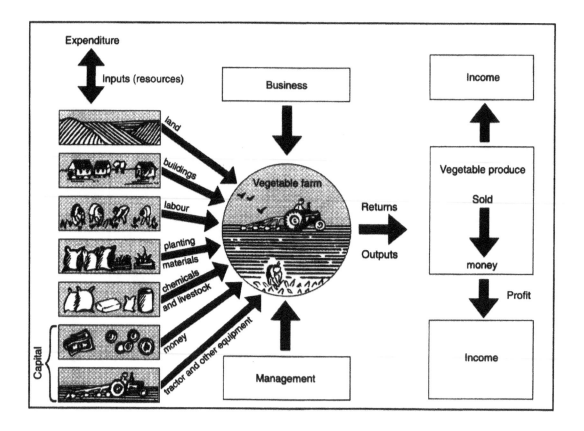

Practical activity

Here is an activity for you to do. Visit a nearby farm.
Carefully observe and take notes on the following.
1 The type of farm
2 The resources or inputs of the farm
3 The outputs of the farm
4 The activities which take place on the farm
On your return, use the notes to complete the table
below.

Type of Farm	Farm inputs (Resources)	Farm Outputs	Farm Activities

Summary

A business is an enterprise in which money is invested in the form of land, buildings, equipment, labour and stock. These items of expenditure are known as inputs or resources and are used to produce goods and services. These are the outputs. From the sales of these outputs, the business makes money which is its income.

In a successful business, the income is greater than the expenditure. As a result the business makes a profit.

A good farmer operates his farm as a business. He ensures that his income is greater than his expenditure, so that the farm operates at a profit.

Remember these

Business	An enterprise established and operated for financial gains.
Expenditure	Money spent on the inputs required in a business enterprise.
Income	Money made from the sale of goods and services.
Inputs (Resources)	Items needed in the establishment and operation of a business.
Manager	The person who operates or manages a business enterprise.
Mixed farm	A farm on which crops are grown and livestocks are reared.
Outputs (Returns)	Goods and services produced for sale.
Profit	The monies realised from a business after deducting the expenditure from the income.
Specialised farm	A farm established to produce items or goods of a special nature, for example, vegetables only or livestocks only.
Stock	Items of goods, produce or livestock for sale.

Do these test exercises

1 Select the best answer from the choices given.

a The main reason for establishing and operating a business enterprise is to:
A provide goods and services to people
B give people employment
C bring financial gains
D help develop the community

b A farmer grows crops and rears livestock. His farm is known as a:
A specialised farm
B mixed farm
C vegetable farm
D livestock farm

c Money, materials and equipment invested in a business enterprise are called:
A inputs
B outputs
C income
D returns

d A farm makes profit when the:
A inputs are equal to the outputs
B inputs are greater than the outputs
C outputs are greater than the inputs
D outputs are less than the inputs

e Herbicides are used in the control of:
A mole crickets
B caterpillars
C fungi
D weeds

2 Fill the blank spaces in the sentences below with words from this list:

management, sale, less, income, business, expenditure, greater, profit.

a A farmer is a businessman because he depends upon his farm to bring him an ....

b .... is the money spent on business resources.

c Income is the money derived from the .... of farm produce.

d A farmer makes a profit when his expenditure is .... than his income.

e A farm operates at a loss when the expenditure is .... than the income.

f A good farmer must have .... and .... skills.

g A successful farm makes a ....

3 Take a walk through your village or a nearby town and make a list of five to ten business enterprises in operation.

4 Complete the table below by inserting the farm activities and farm outputs associated with the listed farm types. An example is done for you.

5 Explain the following in your own words.

a How a farmer obtains his income
b How profit is worked out
c The resources of a business farm
d A skilled labourer

6 What functions do the following farm workers perform?

a the farm manager
b an attendant on a poultry farm
c a worker on a vegetable farm

7 What is the difference between a mixed farm and a specialised farm? Make a list of some specialised farms in your country, e.g. poultry farms.

8 A farmer desires to establish a goat farm. Prepare him a list of (a) the required inputs and (b) the expected outputs of such a farm.

9 A tractor can perform almost every kind of farm labour, yet many farmers do not own tractors. What reasons can you give for this.

Type of farm	Farm activities	Farm outputs
Poultry	brooding chicks caring for broilers and layers, collecting, grading and packing eggs, slaughtering and dressing broiler birds removing litter	live birds, meat, eggs, poultry manure
Dairy		
Pig		

13 Tools and equipment

Lesson objectives

A farmer uses tools and equipment in farm operations. At the end of this lesson you should be able to:

1 identify some of the tools and equipment used in agriculture.

2 state the uses of tools and equipment on a farm.

3 list some factors that should be considered in the selection of tools and equipment.

4 give reasons for the proper care and storage of tools.

5 mention some safety measures that should be exercised in the use of tools and equipment.

How to choose tools and equipment

Mr Devan is looking at a forested piece of land. He wants to set up a mixed farm, that is, a farm on which crops are grown and livestock are reared. He has lands as well as **capital**. He can obtain labour quite easily. All he needs now are tools and equipment.

What kinds of tools and equipment does Mr Devan need? This will depend on the size of his farm and the type of work and activities that will take place there. Small farms need fewer tools and **implements**, which may be simple in structure and design. Large farms will need more costly machines and heavy equipment.

Now consider the following questions:

Is Mr Devan's farm going to be large or small?

What kinds of crops will he grow?

What kinds of animals will he rear?

Will his animals be housed?

How will he get his produce to the markets?

From these questions you will see that Mr Devan needs the following types of tools.

Tools for construction

Tools will be needed for the erection of buildings, and the construction of roads, fences, drains and bridges.

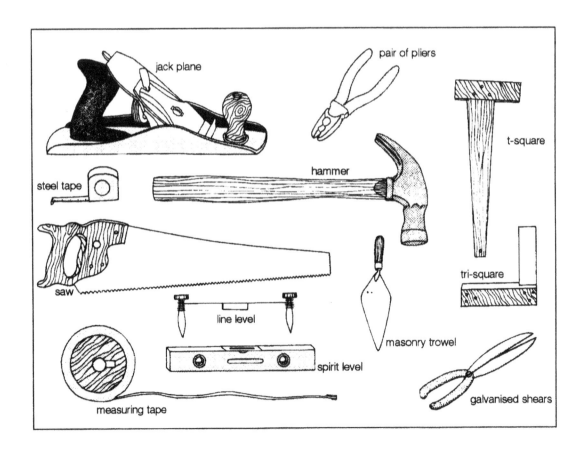

A. Land preparation tools

Measuring tape
Fork
Hoe
Spade
Trowel
Hand fork

B. Nursery and planting tools

Sieve for sifting soil
Seed box
Dibber
Press-board
Clay pots

C. Watering devices

Sprinklers
Watering-can
Bucket
Water-hose

D. Pruning tools

Secateurs
Pruning knife
Garden shears

E. Plant protection

Soil injector
Spray can
Respirator
Duster

F. Harvesting

Knives
Fork
Sickle
Goulet

G. Grading and packaging

Sieve for grading
Packed item
e.g. lettuce in plastic bags

H. Transport

Wheel cart
Basket
Hand box
Wheelbarrow

Tools and equipment for the garden

Several types of tools and equipment are needed in the garden. These include implements for land preparation, **nursery** and planting operations, watering, pruning, plant protection, harvesting, grading and packaging, and transport, (see previous page).

Other equipment for the small farm

Many other types of equipment, such as milking machines, strip cups, scales, incubators, and refrigerators, may be needed on the small farm. The pictures below show some of them.

Equipment on large farms

Large farms require all the tools and equipment of small farms. In addition, they need machinery and tractor-drawn implements like those shown in the pictures on the opposite page.

Refrigerator

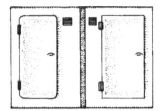

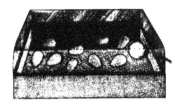

Incubator

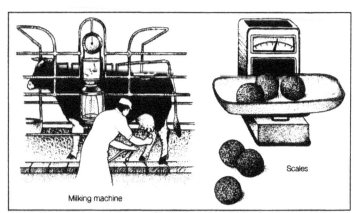

Milking machine

Scales

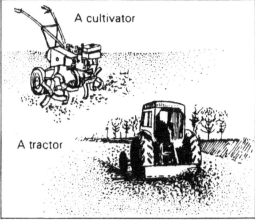

A cultivator

A tractor

How tools work

Tools cannot work by themselves. They need **energy** to make them work. A motor-car gets its energy from petrol and the machines in the metal workshop get their energy from electricity. A hoe or a garden fork must get its power or energy from man.

Now look at the machines or implements at work in the pictures on this page. Find out and say what their energy sources are, and what type of work is being done in each case.

Safe use of tools and equipment

Tools and equipment are essential items on a farm, but they could be harmful if not properly handled and stored.

Here are four important safety measures in the use and storage of tools and equipment.

1 Be careful about yourself and others around you as you carry or use such tools as hoes, cutlasses and forks.
2 Tools with sharp edges should always be at rest on the flat side, while those with pointed tips should be kept standing with the tips on the ground.
3 Safety gear should be worn when spraying against pests and diseases.
4 Tools and equipment that are not in use should be properly stacked and locked in a tool room.

Choice and care of tools

Tools must be chosen with care. They must be suitable for the work that is to be done. Their size, weight and balance must not be more than can be managed by the persons who have to use them.

Tools must be **durable**, that is, they must be able to last for a long time. The metallic parts should be made of bright, smooth, stainless steel. The wooden parts should be of good seasoned wood.

A sharpening file

A single tool can be used for several types of work. It is best for a farmer to buy only the essential tools for his farm.

Even the best tools cannot do good work or last long if they are not treated with care.

Wooden handles should be strong and durable. They should not be too heavy, too short, or too long. All wooden handles should be smooth, as this prevents injury to the hand during work. Handles should be well set and tightly fitted. Blades must be properly ground and sharpened before use.

Tools that are in constant use deteriorate with time. Blades must be sharpened regularly, and broken handles repaired or replaced. It is necessary for all repairs to be done as soon as possible.

Many tools have moving parts. These should be oiled and greased regularly. Damaged packings and rubbers in spray cans must be replaced.

Tools that are exposed to the weather soon become rusty. Do you know why rusting takes place? Leave a cutlass or a fork in a field for five or six days. Then look for rust. Rusting takes place when air and moisture react with iron to form iron oxides or rust.

Now coat your tools with oil or paint. Look for rust again. Can you tell why no rust is formed? It is because the metal is now protected from the action of air and moisture.

We should always protect our tools from rust by coating them periodically with oil, grease or paint.

The storage of tools

Tools cost a lost of money. They should be taken care of. When not in use they should be cleaned, dried, oiled, and neatly stacked in a tool-room. Tools should be put in their own places so that it is easy to collect and check them. This will also help to keep the room tidy.

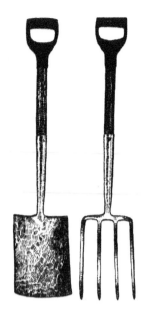

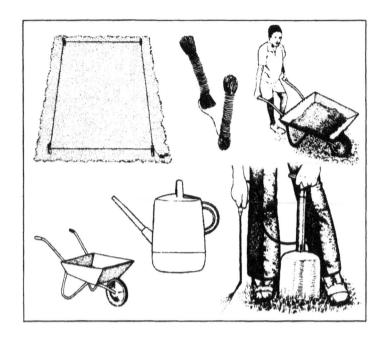

Tools, their purposes and usefulness

Tools serve many useful purposes in the garden. Can you say what are the uses of the tools in the pictures above?

In your class discussions your teacher will tell you more about other garden tools and equipment

Summary

Tools and equipment are essential in farm operations. They may vary from simple hand tools like hammers, forks, spades and shovels to large heavy machines and equipment such as ploughs and rotavators.

Garden tools and equipment are usually classified or grouped according to the purposes for which they are used. For example, hammers, saws and jackplanes are used for construction and grouped as construction tools. In like manner, there are tools and equipment for land preparation, nursery and planting operations, watering, **pruning**, plant protection, harvesting, grading and packaging, storage and transport.

Other useful types of equipment are milking machines and **incubators**. These are used on farm animals.

Farmers should select their tools and equipment with care, and maintain them properly. Tools should be strong, durable and suitable for the work that is to be done. They should be sharpened regularly, repaired or have worn out parts replaced, oiled or greased periodically and they should be stacked in a tool room after use.

It must be remembered, too, that tools and equipment could be harmful to the persons using them and to others around. Care and safety should be exercised at all times in the handling, usage and storage of tools.

Remember these

Capital   Finance or money for investment in a business enterprise.

Durable   Can last for a long time.

Energy   Power to do work.

Harrow   An agricultural implement used for breaking up clumps of soil into small particles.

Implement   A tool for doing work. For example a plough.

Incubator   An equipment for hatching eggs artificially.

Nursery   Plants in the seedling stage.

Prune   The act of removing unwanted shoots or branches.

Rust   A brown dusty substance or oxide formed from the reaction of air and moisture on the surface of a metal such as iron.

Sieve   An apparatus used for separating finer particles from coarser ones.

Practical activities

Here are two practical activities for you to do.

1 Take a garden fork, a garden spade, and a short-handled cutlass and find the following particulars.
   a total length including handle
   b length of handle alone
   c total weight

Use the information to complete the table below.

Tool	Total length (nearest cm of in)	Length of handle alone (nearest cm or in)	Total weight (nearest kg or lb)
Garden fork			
Garden spade			
Short handle cutlass			
Garden trowel			

2 Go to a hardware store and estimate the cost of the tools listed on page 96.

Tool	Estimated Cost	
	$	¢
Garden spade		
Garden trowel		
Garden line		
Hammer		
Pruning knife		
Light garden fork		
Draw hoe		
Saw (rip)		
Watering can		
Spirit level		
Total		

Do these test exercises

1 Select the best answer from the choices given.

a A farmer has capital for developing his farm. This means that he has money:
   A derived from the sale of farm produce
   B to invest in his agricultural programme
   C kept as savings in the bank
   D taken on loan for a period of tim

b Which group of tools is best suited for plant protection:
   A fork, spade, hoe
   B secateurs, wheel barrow, trowel
   C duster, mist blower, soil injector
   D sieve, seed box, press board

c A plough is used for:
   A breaking up soil clumps
   B digging the soil
   C forming garden plots
   D clearing lands for cultivation

d Rusting of tools could be avoided by:
   A selecting tools made from steel
   B keeping them stacked in a tool room
   C using them only under dry conditions
   D oiling and greasing the metal parts

hammer

e The tool in the picture above is best suited for work in:
   A construction
   B land preparation
   C nursery production
   D plant protection

2 Fill the blank spaces in the sentences below with suitable words selected from this list.

moisture, construction, greased, equipment, energy, durable, wheel barrow, oiled, incubator, suitable, rusting, electricity, products.

a Tools need .... to make them work.

b .... is a source of energy.

c Eggs are hatched artificially in an ....

d Tools with moving parts should be .... and .... regularly.

e The reaction of air and .... on iron metal cause ....

f A .... is used for transporting materials on a farm.

g Tools must be strong, ... and .... for the work that is to be done.

3 Give good reasons why:

a tools should be sharpened regularly

b wooden handles should be smooth

c tools should be oiled periodically

d moving parts of machines should be greased

4 List the tools and equipment needed for:

a pruning a rose plant

b constructing a poultry shed

c planting a citrus tree

d sanitation on a dairy farm

5 Why do garden tools rust? How would you prevent this?

14 The plant and its environment

Lesson objectives

There are several environmental factors which affect plant growth and production. Among these, soil is a major factor. On completing this lesson you should be able to:

1 name the environmental factors which affect plants and plant growth.

2 list the ways in which the soil supports plants.

3 name the chief components of the soil.

4 describe the processes of soil formation.

5 explain the role of soil organisms in improving soil fertility.

6 differentiate between topsoil and subsoil.

7 explain the concepts of soil texture and soil structure.

8 demonstrate the presence of air and water in the soil by means of experiments.

9 perform an experiment to determine the kinds of particles present in a given soil type.

10 identify the three major soil types: clay, loam and sand.

11 list three features which characterise each of the three major soil types.

The plant and its environment

Mr John cultivates bananas in his home garden. Let us find out more about the environment in which his bananas grow. Study the picture and consider the following questions.

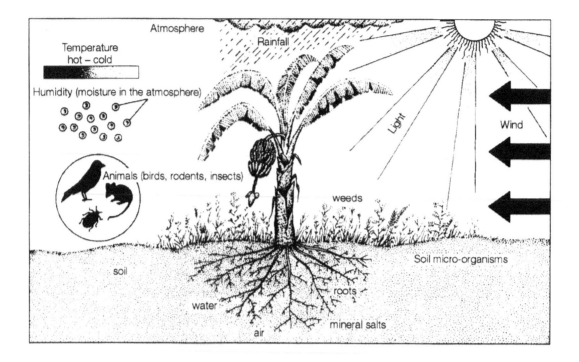

The root

Where does the root of the banana grow?

What does the root get from the soil?

Are soil organisms important?

Roots grow and develop in the soil. They breathe air and absorb water and mineral salts. These are essential for plant growth. Several types of organisms are present in the soil. Many of them are useful while some of them are harmful.

The shoot

Where does the shoot grow?

What factors affect the shoot?

Study the picture carefully. You will observe that the banana shoot is exposed to light, temperature, wind movements, rainfall and humidity. These are atmospheric or climatic factors. The shoot is also surrounded by plant and animal organisms such as weeds, birds, rodents and insects. These are living things and known as the biotic factors of the **environment**.

The chief environmental factors affecting our plants are soil, climate and other living organisms.

The chart opposite will help you to understand this better.

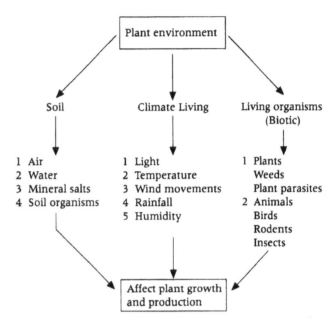

The soil

We have seen that the soil is the chief environment in which the roots of plants grow and develop. Collect a shovel of garden soil and look at it carefully.

What is the colour of the soil?

Is it loose or lumpy?

Is it smooth or gritty?

Can it hold water?

Is the soil 'alive' or 'dead'?

Soil content

Soil air

Use a drinking straw and blow some air through it into a jar of water. What do you see? Bubbles, of course. These are air bubbles moving to the water's surface.

Now take a clod of very dry soil and immerse it in a jar of water. Do you see air bubbles rising out of the soil? These bubbles tell us that the soil contains air.

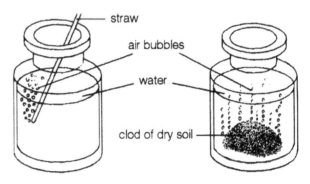

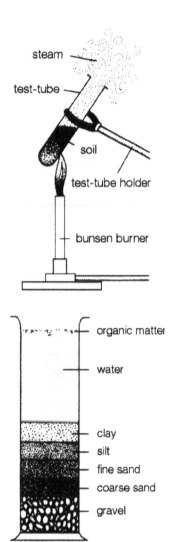

Soil water

Heat some soil in a test tube. Watch the steam escaping from it. Place a mirror over the steam. What do you notice? Why does the surface of the mirror become cloudy? Now test for water with blue cobalt chloride paper. Remember that water turns blue cobalt chloride paper pink. This experiment tells us that soil contains water.

Soil solids

Put some garden soil in the bottom of a measuring cylinder or jar. Add water and shake vigorously. Allow the cylinder or jar to settle.

Notice the layers of different kinds of solids formed at the bottom of the jar. These solids are derived from rocks and are the **inorganic** soil particles. Floating on the surface of the water are the **organic** soil particles. These are derived from the decay of plants and animals.

The inorganic soil particles

The inorganic soil particles are rich in minerals and supply the plants with their nutrient requirements. These particles vary in size and are named accordingly, for example:

Soil particles	Gravel	Coarse sand	Fine sand	Silt	Clay
Diameter (mm)	above	between	between	between	less than
	2.0	2.0–0.2	0.2–0.02	0.02–0.002	0.002

The amount and kinds of inorganic particles in a soil form the soil texture.

The way in which these particles are put together to form an **aggregate**, that is a lump of soil, is known as the soil structure.

The organic soil particles

The organic particles decompose to form humus in the soil. They supply foods for soil organisms and nutrients to our plants. Organic matter binds sand particles and separates clays. It absorbs and retains water in the soil.

Soil organisms

Rodent

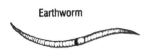

Earthworm

There are several types of soil organisms. Some are macroscopic, that is, they could be seen with the naked eye. These include the roots of plants, insects, snails, slugs, millipedes, earthworms and small mammals. Others like fungi, bacteria and nematodes could only be seen under a microscope and these are said to be microscopic. The activities of these organisms help to increase soil fertility by improving aeration and water movement in the soil. Fungi and bacteria decompose and mineralise organic matter from which plant foods are derived. Nematodes are often harmful to our plants.

We have seen that soil is composed of air, water, organic and inorganic solids, and soil organisms. These are the chief components of the soil mixed together to make our garden soil.

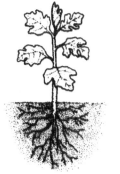

Plant roots

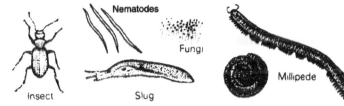

Nematodes

Fungi

Millipede

Insect

Slug

Topsoil and subsoil

The picture on page 102 shows you the cut edge of a newly made road on a hillside. What you see is a **soil profile**, that is, a picture of the soil from the surface where plants grow to the rocks below. The first 20–30 cm of surface soil is called **topsoil** and below this is the **subsoil**.

The topsoil is generally dark in colour because of the presence of organic matter. It is also better aerated than the subsoil and contains an abundance of plant roots and soil organisms.

The subsoil, however, is rocky in nature. It is more compact, less aerated and contains less organic matter than the topsoil.

Now say why (a) plant roots and soil organisms are found more abundantly in the topsoil than in the subsoil and (b) crops cultivated on topsoil grow better and give higher yields than crops cultivated on subsoil.

A soil profile

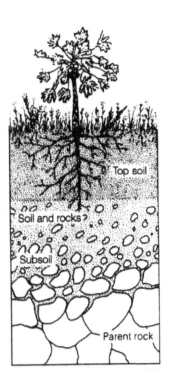

Top soil

Soil and rocks?

Subsoil

Parent rock

How soils are formed

Soils are formed by the weathering of rocks and by the activities of living organisms. This is a continuing process.

Weathering of rocks

The chief agents of weathering are wind, water and the changes of temperature. Winds lift particles of sand and soil and deposit them against rocks causing them to wear down into small fragments and fine particles.

The force of raindrops upon rocks or the rolling of rocks by moving water wears the rocks down physically into smaller fragments and particles. Water also acts chemically by dissolving soluble substances in the rocks causing them to crack and fall apart.

These actions continue and the rock particles finally break down into soil.

Temperature varies between day and night and between seasons. In the day when it is hot rocks expand; at night when it is cold they contract. This expansion and contraction causes the outer surface of rocks to crumble and fall to the ground. During the cold months, water in the cracks of rocks freezes and expands. The cracks become larger and the rocks split open and fall apart.

Over a period of time, these rock particles continue to break down to form soil.

Activities of living organisms

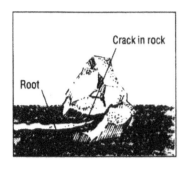

Living organisms like plants, soil microbes and even man help in the formation of soil. The roots of plants grow in the cracks of rocks. As they develop and push their way into the cracks, the rocks split open and finally break down.

Soil microbes act upon the remains of plants and animals. Soon these substances decompose to form humus in the soil.

Man also assists in soil formation. He digs and ploughs the soil, in so doing the rocks are broken into smaller fragments and finally into soil.

Soils and soil conditions

Crops are generally grown on three major soil types. These are clays, loams and sand.

Clays

Clays are composed of tiny particles and are generally rich in plant nutrients. They have small or capillary pore spaces, that is, the spaces between the particles which retain soil water. Clays become easily water logged and are often heavy and difficult to work.

To avoid waterlogging, clayey soils must be tilled and well drained. This helps to grow good crops.

Loams

Loams are a mixture of clays and sands. They are rich in nutrients, easily drained and well aerated. They are light and easy to work.

Loams are generally considered the best soils for growing crops.

Sands

Sand particles are larger than those of clays. Sands have large pore spaces which do not hold water but are filled with air. They are also very poor in nutrient supplies. The addition of organic matter helps to bind sand and retain water. Fertilisers are also needed to improve the nutrient content of sandy soils in order to produce good crops.

In another book you will learn more about cultivating the soil for crop production.

Summary

Plants are exposed to three major environmental factors. These are soil, weather conditions or climate and living organisms of various types. The soil accommodates the roots of plants and supplies them with air, water and mineral salts.

The soil is made up of several substances. These include air, water, inorganic and organic solids and soil organisms. The inorganic substances are derived from weathered rocks whilst the organic compounds are formed from the decomposition of plants and animals. These two components are the most important sources of plant nutrient in the soil.

There are several types of soil organisms. Some of them are macroscopic and others are microscopic. These organisms help to increase soil fertility by improving aeration and water movement in the soil and by hastening the process of organic decomposition and mineralisation.

The upper 20–30 cm of the soil's profile is known as the topsoil. Below this is the subsoil. The topsoil is generally rich in organic matter. It is well aerated and well populated with useful soil micro-organisms. It is on the topsoil that most of our agriculture is done.

Soils are formed from the breaking down of rocks by the agents of weathering and by the activities of living organisms. The decomposition of organic matter into humus adds to the soil during the process of soil formation.

There are three major soil types on which crops are grown. These are clays, loams and sand. Clays are composed of very fine particles and capillary pore spaces. It is rich in minerals but tends to become waterlogged. Sands are made up of large particles with large pore spaces which do not hold water. It is also poor in nutrient supplies. Loams are a mixture of sand and clays and these are our best soils on which to grow crops.

Remember these

Capillary pore spaces   Very small pore spaces in the soil which hold water.

Environment	The conditions and influences which surround a person or object.
Inorganic substances	Substances derived from materials such as rocks which do not belong to the plant and animal kingdom.
Macroscopic soil organism	Soil organisms that could be seen with the naked eye.
Microscopic soil organisms	Soil organisms that could be seen only under a microscope.
Organic substances	Substances formed from the decay of plants and animals.
Soil aggregates	Clumps of soil varying in size and shape.
Soil profile	A vertical cross section of the soil showing different layers or beds of soil formation.
Soil structure	The way in which soil particles are arranged to form an aggregate.
Soil texture	The type and amount of inorganic particles in a soil.

Practical activities

1 Collect a sample of soil from four different areas in your village. Label them S1, S2, S3 and S4.
  Make observations on the samples collected. State the following:
  Sample S1
  a date of collection
  b place where collected
  c weather condition at the time of collection
  d was it topsoil or subsoil
  e the colour of the soil
  f the feel of the soil
  g the type of soil sampled
2 Take a clod of very dry soil and immerse it in a jar of water. State your observations. This is an experiment. Write it up as follows:

Name of experiment	e.g. an experiment to show that soil contains air
Apparatus and materials	State all the apparatus and materials you will use
Procedure	State how you will go about doing the experiment
Observations	State your observations
Conclusion	Write down your conclusion from what you have observed

Now do this experiment again using a very wet clod of soil. State reasons for any differences in your observations.

3 Place some soil in a test tube and heat over a bunsen burner. Test for the presence of moisture (water) using a mirror or blue cobalt chloride paper.

Write up your experiment using the guide given in question 2 above.

4 Collect about 250–300 g of garden soil and crush it. Place the crushed soil in a jar three quarter filled with water and shake vigorously. Allow the jar to settle for a period of twelve hours.

Make a drawing showing the layers and label it. What information do you get about the soil from this experiment.

5 Look at the cut edge of a newly made road on a hillside. Make a drawing of the soil profile showing the topsoil and the subsoil.

Do these test exercises

1 Consider these statements carefully. State whether they are *true or false*.

a Inorganic soil particles are derived from rocks.

b Fine sand is the smallest inorganic soil particle.

c More plant roots are found in the subsoil than in the topsoil.

d Fungi and bacteria are microscopic soil organisms.

e Clays are more readily drained than loams.

2 Select the best answer from the choices given.

a A biotic factor affecting plant growth and development is
A insect
B wind
C rainfall
D temperature

b Which of these is a microscopic soil organism?
A earthworm
B lizard
C bacterium
D millipede

c Organic matter is decomposed by soil organisms to form:
A clay
B humus
C silt
D loam

d Capillary soil water is found most abundantly in the pore spaces of:
A sands
B loams
C silt
D clays

e Soil texture refers to:
A the arrangement of soil particles to form an aggregate
B the size of the pore spaces in the soil
C the amount and type of particles in a soil
D the appearance of the soil after it is ploughed and tilled

3 List the components which make up the soil.

4 State the difference between organic and inorganic substances present in the soil.

5 Explain how the soil is improved by:
a the addition of organic matter
b the construction of drains
c the activities of soil organisms

6 List four agents of soil formation.

7 Explain why:
a The movement of water in clays is very slow whilst the movement of water in sands is very rapid
b Loams are our best agricultural soils

8 Write a short paragraph saying why "the topsoil is best suited for agriculture".

15 Climate and agriculture

Lesson objectives

The major climatic factors affecting plants are rainfall, temperature, humidity, light and wind movements. These factors relate to weather conditions and they have considerable effects on crops and crop production practices. On completing this lesson you should be able to:

1 list the climatic factors which affect crops and crop production practices.

2 differentiate between climate and weather.

3 describe how weather conditions affect crops and crop production practices

4 read weather instruments and make recordings.

5 demonstrate the effect of climatic factors by means of experiments.

6 explain why crops and crop production practices change with altitude.

In the last lesson you learnt that the major climatic factors affecting plants are rainfall, temperature, humidity, light and wind movements.

These factors relate to weather conditions which vary from place to place and from one season to another. In the Caribbean there are two major seasons – the wet season, lasting from June to December, and the dry season, from January to May. Climatic factors are measured and expressed in several ways. However, when we speak about the 'climate' of a place we refer to the average weather conditions over a certain period of time. Such a period is never less than ten years.

How does climate affect agriculture? Look at the farmers around and you will notice that they do not grow the same crops all the year round. Under natural conditions tomatoes and cabbages are planted mostly in the dry season, and rice is planted in the rainy or wet season. This is so because these crops thrive best under those weather conditions.

Now find answers for the following.

Why is sugar cane harvested in the dry season?

Why is milk yield greater in the wet season than in the dry season?

Why is it difficult to grow wheat in tropical conditions?

Rainfall

Rain is our primary water source

The rain is our primary water source. Farmers need water for their crops and animals. Many factories and processing units also require water in their manufacturing processes.

Wait for the next shower of rain and make the following observations:

How long did the shower last?

Was the shower light or heavy?

How much water fell in that shower of rain?

Was that shower enough for our crops and animals?

Farmers need just enough rain, falling gently over a sufficiently long period of time. Heavy rains are disastrous to crops. Can you say why? They beat down the flowers from fruit trees, erode the land and cause floods.

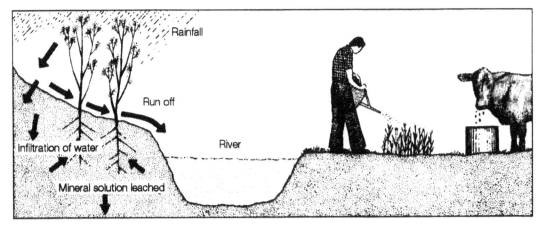

What happens to our rainfall?

If you watch a shower of rain you will notice that some of the raindrops fall on the leaves of plants and some fall on the ground.

The raindrops that fall on the leaves help to keep the leaves cool. Some of the water evaporates from the surface of the leaves while some drips slowly to the ground to increase the soil water.

When it is too wet, the leaves may be attacked by fungus diseases. This happens because many fungi live and thrive best under damp conditions.

The raindrops which fall on the exposed ground may infiltrate or run off. The water which infiltrates is very beneficial to the plant, as it dissolves minerals in the soil to form soil solutions which are absorbed by the roots of the plants. In sandy or porous soils soluble mineral substances are easily leached out.

Water moistens the soil and makes it easy to cultivate. It helps germination and helps the roots of plants to grow deeper and further into the soil in search of plant food.

Surface run off goes to form rivers and lakes. These are reservoirs from which water is obtained for domestic and irrigation purposes. When there are heavy showers, surface run off erodes the land, silts up rivers, and causes floods which damage crops and livestock.

Remember

Rainfall is measured in millimetres by means of a rain gauge. In nature there is a water-cycle. You will study these in your General Science Classes.

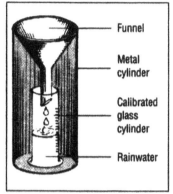

Funnel

Metal cylinder

Calibrated glass cylinder

Rainwater

Rain gauge

Temperature

What is the temperature in your classroom?
Is it hot or cold?
If you want to find out the temperature, that is, how hot or cold it is, you can measure this with a thermometer. This is an instrument calibrated in degrees centigrade (°C) which tells you how hot or cold the atmosphere is. Take a reading of the temperature of your classroom in the morning and one later in the afternoon. Was there a change of temperature? If so, what reason can you give for this?

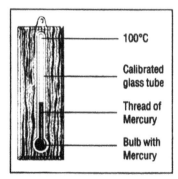

100°C

Calibrated glass tube

Thread of Mercury

Bulb with Mercury

Thermometer

The influence of temperature on plants

Temperature affects plant growth in several ways. The major effects, however, are those on germination of seeds, transpiration and evaporation.

Temperature and germination of seeds

Take some freshly collected bean seeds and sow them in three seed boxes to germinate under different conditions.

Seed box No. 1   Boil the seeds, then sow them in the box to germinate

Seed box No. 2   Sow the seeds to germinate and place the box in a refrigerator

Seed box No. 3   Sow the seeds to germinate and place the box in the nursery shed.

Give the three boxes the same treatment, that is, gently water them every day.

State your observations after 7–10 days.

  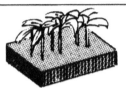

No. 1 Boiled seed.   No. 2 Seed from refrigerator.   No. 3 Seed in nursery shed.

Which seeds germinated?

Which did not? Why?

How did boiling affect the seeds in seed box No. 1?

How did refrigeration affect the seeds in seed box No. 2?

Why did the seeds in seed box No. 3 germinate?

The boiled seeds were affected by high temperatures whereas the seeds placed in the refrigerator were affected by very cold temperatures. From this exercise you can see that very high or very cold temperatures affect germination or plant growth.

Temperature and transpiration

Plants give off water from their leaves, this is called transpiration. On hot days, leaves transpire excessively

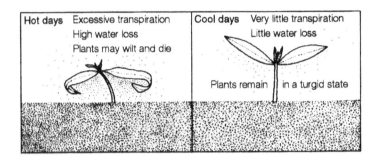

and the plants may wilt. On cool or cloudy days there is less transpiration and wilting does not occur.

Can you say why:

transpiration is excessive on hot days,

there is less transpiration on cloudy days,

wilting occurs on hot days?

High temperatures lead to excessive transpiration. The water-loss in plants is great, and wilting occurs.

Temperature and evaporation

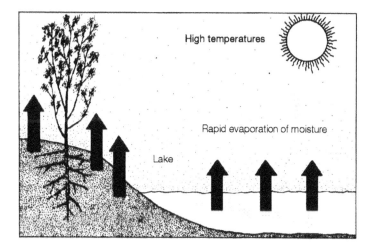

Evaporation of moisture

On hot days more evaporation takes place from land and water surfaces. In the absence of rainfall and irrigation the soil water becomes depleted and the plants wilt and die.

Temperature and altitude

In some territories there are arable land (lands on which agriculture is done) at high altitudes such as lands on the slopes and valleys of the Blue Mountains in Jamaica and on the Aripo heights of the Northern Range in Trinidad. With the rise in altitude, that is, height above sea level, there is a fall in temperature, and this factor influences the type of crops that could be grown and the production practices that should be adopted in farming done at high altitudes.

Remember this

Many plants grow and thrive best at their particular temperature ranges. Very high or very low temperatures restrict the growth and activities of plants, and may even cause them to die. Flowering, fertilisation, and fruit formation may all be affected by temperature changes.

Humidity

Take a glass with some ice-cubes in it and place it on a table.

Notice the condensation of moisture which takes place on the outer surface of the glass. What does this tell you? It tells you that water vapour is present in the air.

Saturation point

The air holds water vapour. At saturation point, the air cannot hold any more water vapour.

Relative humidity

At any specific temperature, the air may contain less water vapour than it could hold at saturation point. The ratio between the water vapour present in the air and the quantity it would hold if it were saturated is known as the 'relative humidity'.

Relative humidity is found from the difference in the readings of a dry and wet bulb. A great difference in the readings indicates that the air is dry. Air with a relative humidity of 85 per cent and more is considered damp, while 60 per cent and under is considered very dry.

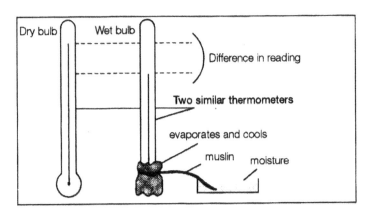

Humidity and agriculture

At low humidity there is greater evaporation and more rapid transpiration. Wilting takes place, especially in young plants and seedlings. Under this condition surface mulching and more frequent watering are necessary.

When the humidity is high there is little evaporation and transpiration. However, damp conditions favour fungal growth, diseases become prevalent and spray control measures may be needed.

Light

Plants need light

Take a potted plant and place it on your window sill. Observe it for seven to eight days. Notice how the plant grows towards the light. This tells you that the plant needs light.

Why do plants need light?

Plants need light for normal growth. Light is necessary for chlorophyll development and to give the plant rigidity. Light is also essential in photosynthesis, that is, in the manufacture of sugars and starches. Energy is needed in the process and the plant absorbs its energy from light.

Too much light and too little light are both bad for the plant. What the plant needs is the optimum amount of light, that is, the right quantity of light for healthy plant growth.

Do all plants need the same amount of light?

Many people grow plants inside their homes. Do these plants get the same amount of light as the plants that grow in open fields? They certainly don't. From this observation we gather that some plants need more light than others.

Plants that need plenty of sunlight are called sun-loving plants. Those that need little or less light are called shade-loving plants. Are your house plants shade-loving or sun-loving plants?

These grew in the light

These grew in the dark

Light and field plants

Field crops need plenty of light. How can a farmer ensure that his crops are getting enough light? Land should be properly cleared, plants adequately spaced and garden plots kept free from weeds. These will all help our garden crops to get sufficient light. Some field plants like the cocoa may need a reduced amount of light. Such plants may be provided with overhead shade trees like the immortelle.

Wind

How winds are formed

Observe the trees on a windy day. Notice how they bend. This indicates that the wind is a powerful agent. How are winds formed? The diagram will help you to understand this. When the direct rays of the sun strike on a land mass the earth becomes heated creating a region of low pressure. The hot air expands, becomes light and rises, whilst cold heavy air or winds rush to take its place.

Direct rays of the sun

Cold heavy air

Rising hot air

Cold heavy air

Heated land mass

Low pressure region

Wet and dry winds

Winds may be wet or dry. Wet winds are moisture laden and they tend to deposit moisture. These winds are important to the farmer as they bring rainfall which is essential for the growth of the crops. Dry winds lack moisture. When they blow over the land they tend to absorb moisture. These winds may be harmful to our plants as they dry up the land and cause droughts.

How winds affect our crops

Winds are helpful in some ways and harmful in many others. Light or gentle breezes may be helpful to our plants. They blow pollen grains and assist in the process of pollination.
Why is pollination important?
Does it help to increase fruit and crop production?
What does increased fruit and crop production mean to the farmer? Have you seen the wind blowing away soil

Trees and grasses are planted to prevent exposure of the topsoil

particles? On open land where the soil is loose the wind blows surface soil away and piles it to form sand hills.

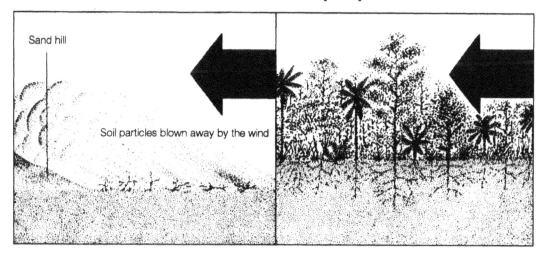

Sand hill

Soil particles blown away by the wind

What do you call the loss of surface soils? Why is the loss of surface soils harmful to our lands and crops?

Wind erosion should be avoided. This could be done by preventing land from becoming exposed. Trees and grasses are planted so that their roots will help to bind the soil.

Pastures should never be over-grazed. Can you say why? Dairy farmers carry on a rotational grazing programme, that is, the animals are moved from one paddock to another in a rotational scheme. As a result the pastures are never over-grazed.

Winds may do physical damage to our crops. They break branches, and blow down flowers and fruits. Shallow rooted crops like banana may be completely uprooted resulting in the loss of trees and bunches of fruits.

Winds spoil the shape of trees. In the photograph over-leaf you will observe that more branches are on the

Direction of the wind

leeward side than on the windward side. In the course of time the trees become heavy on the leeward side resulting in the breakage of branches and the uprooting of trees.

Protecting our garden crops from the wind

In windswept areas farmers protect their crops by establishing wind breaks. Look at the picture below and you will notice that a barrier of trees is established on the windward side of the garden that is cultivated with crops. When the wind strikes the barrier, the force of the wind is broken and its course is deflected, so the wind passes over the crops without causing damage.

Summary

Climate is defined as the average weather condition over a period of time. The chief climatic factors affecting plants and plant production are rainfall, temperature, humidity, light and wind movements.

Rainfall is our main source of water supply. Water is needed for domestic and commercial purposes and for irrigating farm lands. Rain water penetrates and softens

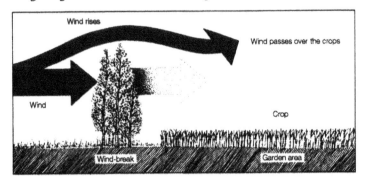

the soil, making it easy for root development and for work. It also dissolves mineral substances to form soil solutions which are absorbed by the roots of plants. During heavy rainfall there is excessive run-off. This causes erosion and flooding which damage crops and livestock.

Rainfall is essential in agriculture, but there must be just enough, falling gently over a sufficiently long period.

Temperature is measured by a thermometer which tells how hot or cold it is. The major effects of temperature on plants are those on seed germination, transpiration and evaporation. Temperature varies with altitudes. The changes in temperature influence the type of crops grown and the production practices pursued at different altitudes.

Very high or very low temperatures are harmful to crops. What is needed is an optimum temperature, that is, the most suitable temperature for the crops grown.

Humidity relates to the presence of moisture or water vapour in the atmosphere. When the humidity is low there is excess transpiration in plants and evaporation of soil water. However, high humidity favours fungal growth, and diseases become prevalent.

Light is essential for normal plant growth. It is needed for chlorophyll development and for the energy required by plants during the process of photosynthesis. Plants vary in their light requirements. For example, house plants are shade-loving and can thrive on less light than field crops which are sun-loving. For healthy plant growth there must be an optimum amount of light which may vary in the requirements of different crops.

The wind is a very powerful agent. It develops and moves as a result of differences in atmospheric pressures. Winds may be wet or dry. Dry winds tend to pick up moisture whilst wet winds tend to deposit moisture. Heavy winds are dangerous. They may cause erosion on exposed lands and damage to field crops. In windswept areas wind breaks are established to protect crops.

Remember these

Climate	The average weather condition over a certain period.
Dry winds	Winds which tend to pick up moisture.
Humidity	The presence of moisture in the atmosphere.
Infiltration	The downward movement of water into the soil.

Optimum temperature	The most suitable temperature.
Rain gauge	An instrument for measuring rainfall.
Saturation point	The point at which the air could hold no more moisture.
Temperature	The degree of hot or cold as shown by the thermometer.
Thermometer	An instrument for measuring the degree of hot or cold.
Wet winds	Winds which tend to deposit moisture.

Practical activities

1 Read and record the daily temperatures of your classroom at two different points in time during the day over a seven day period. Complete the table below.

Day	Temperature at 9.00 am	Temperature at 2.00 pm	Difference in temperature
1			
2			

a Find the average daily temperatures at (a) 9.00 am and (b) 2.00 pm.

b What is the difference between the average daily temperature at 9.00 am and 2.00 pm. What reason can you give for the difference in temperature?

2 From your school rain gauge read and record the rainfall at 8.00 am daily over seven days and complete the table below.

Day	Time	Rainfall in mm
1		
2		

a What was the total rainfall over the seven day period?

b What was the average daily rainfall?

c On which day was (a) the highest rainfall and (b) the lowest rainfall?

3 Sow some bean seeds in two pots and place one in the light and the other in a dark room. Allow them to germinate and grow for a period of 8–10 days. Now observe them carefully, and record what you see, by copying the table below and filling it in.

Observations	Colour of plant	Size of leaf	Height of plant	Rigidity of plant
Plants grown in the light				
Plants grown in the dark				

What is the colour of plants that grow in the presence of light? What gives the plant this green colour?

What is the colour of plants which grow in the dark?

What do these plants lack?

Which plants have better formed leaves?

Which plants tend to grow taller?

Which plants are more rigid?

Which plants show normal growth?

What do you think would happen if you take the plants that were growing in the dark and now place them to continue their growth in the light?

Do these test exercises

1 Consider these statements carefully. State whether they are true or false.

a Light is a source of energy

b Most fungi live and thrive best under dry conditions

c Plants wilt because there is a shortage of water in their system

d A wind break should be established on the windward side of a garden.

e The higher the reading on the thermometer, the cooler it is.

2 Select the best answer from the choices given.

a Fred read the thermometer in his classroom. He wanted to find out
A the amount of light
B the temperature
C the relative humidity
D the wind movement

b When the farmer spoke about erosion, he was referring to:
A the movement of water in the soil
B the run off of water down a slope
C the removal of surface soil by water
D the retention of water in the soil

c The term "saturation point" is associated with:
A temperature
B humidity
C rainfall
D light

d Winds develop as a result of differences in:
A atmospheric pressures
B rainfall
C temperature
D relative humidity

e The dry season is generally between the months of:
A May to July
B August to October
C November to December
D January to April

3 Complete the sentences below by filling the blank spaces with a suitable word from the bracket at the end of the sentence.

a The normal growth of plants takes place in the .... of light. (presence, absence)

b Wet winds tend to .... moisture. (absorb, deposit)

c Erosion is greater on .... than on .... (low lands, hillsides)

d The green pigment in the leaves of a plant is known as .... (photosynthesis, chlorophyll)

e When the air cannot hold any more water vapour, it is said to be .... (dry, saturated)

4 Give reasons why:

a plants are sprayed against fungal diseases more frequently in the wet season than in the dry season

b trees should be planted on hillsides

c pastures should not be overgrazed

d soil erosion should be prevented

e there is more leaching in sandy soils than in clayey soils

5 Say how the following weather conditions could be harmful to our plants.

Heavy rainfalls, strong winds, drought periods, high humid conditions.

6 Explain how a wind break helps to protect crops.

16 The biotic factors of the environment

Lesson objectives

The biotic factors of the environment relate to living organisms. These include weeds, insects, fungi, bacteria, nematodes and other living creatures. On completing the lesson you should be able to:

1 name the biotic factors of the environment which affect plants.

2 identify an insect.

3 classify insects according to their action on plants.

4 draw an insect and label the parts of its body.

5 differentiate between complete and incomplete metamorphosis.

6 recognise some harmful weeds.

7 describe the methods of controlling weeds, insect pests and plant diseases.

8 explain the concept of integrated pest management.

9 describe the role of soil organisms in improving soil conditions.

You remember that the biotic factors of the environment relate to living organisms. In this section we will study some of these organisms which affect our crops and animals. These include weeds, insects, fungi, bacteria, nematodes and other living creatures.

Weeds

What is a weed?

Mr Collin is spraying the weeds in his banana plot. The crop cultivated is banana. All other plants on the plot are weeds. Weeds are plants that are not wanted where they happen to be growing.

Spraying weeds

How weeds harm our crops

Weeds compete with cultivated plants for soil water and nutrient supplies. They also compete for air and light that are essential for healthy plant growth. Weeds often harbour animals and insects that are harmful to crops. If overgrown, weeds give our garden plots a very untidy appearance.

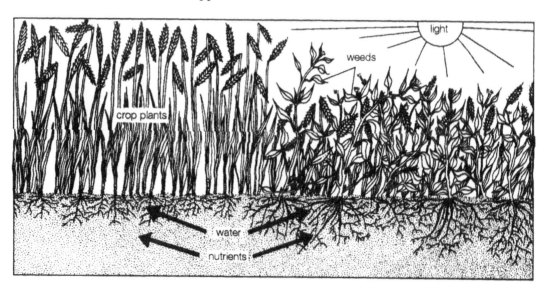

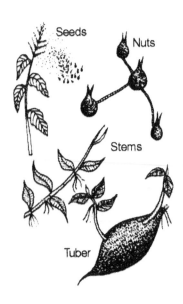

Seeds
Nuts
Stems
Tuber

How weeds are spread

Look at a plot that was ploughed two days ago. You may see few or no weeds on it. Look at the plot again after a period of ten to twelve weeks.

Do you see weeds growing on the plot?

Are there more weeds present than when you first looked at the plot? How did the weeds get to the plot?

Weeds are spread by seeds or by other vegetative parts of the plant. Weeds grow from seeds that probably fell on the garden plot from a previous weed growth or may have been blown in by the wind from some other weedy area. Weed seeds may also be brought in by manures or by the droppings of birds and other animals that feed on grasses and other garden crops. Weeds often grow from bits of green stem that may have been ploughed into the soil, or from root-tubers and corms.

How weeds are controlled

Weeds are controlled by mechanical means. Weeding, brush-cutting and ploughing are all mechanical, the use of sprays such as weedicides and herbicides are chemical.

Some common weeds

The pictures below show you some common weeds found in the Caribbean. Their common names may vary from place to place. Their Latin names are the same everywhere. Try to find them in your school compound.

Fowlfoot grass *Eusine indica*

Para grass *Brachiaria mutica*

Nut grass *Cyperus rotundus*

Corn grass *Rottboellia exaltata*

Bahama grass *Cynodon dactylon*

Water grass *Commelina elegans*

Shame bush *Mimosa pudica*

Railway daisy *Bidens pilosa*

Shame bush *Mimosa pudica*

Amaranthus *Amaranthus dubius*

(Sweetheart) *Desmodium frutescens*

Amaranthus *Amaranthus dubius*

Insects

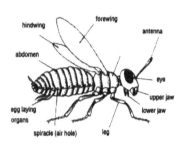

hindwing forewing antenna
abdomen
eye
upper jaw
egg laying lower jaw
organs
spiracle (air hole) leg

Insects are found everywhere. They inhabit hot lands and cold lands. They are found in the air, the soil, the sea, rivers, homes and offices. Some insects are useful, for example, bees pollinate flowers and make honey, and the silkworm spins silk. Others are harmful. Some of them, like roaches, damage clothes in wardrobes and termites tunnel into wooden buildings.

Name an insect which (a) cuts down garden plants and (b) stings when disturbed.

How to recognise an insect

Can you identify an insect? All insects are similar in structure. They only show characteristic differences. Look at a mole cricket or a jack spaniard closely.

The body is divided in three main parts, namely the head, the chest (or thorax) and the abdomen.

The head consists of the eyes, the antennae (feelers) and the mouth parts. Attached to the chest or thorax are two pairs of wings and three pairs of jointed legs. The abdomen, the largest of the three body parts, is segmented and contains the spiracles or pores by which the insect breathes.

Stages of an insect (metamorphosis)

Insects are reproduced by their parents. They undergo several changes before they become adults. These changes are known as metamorphosis.

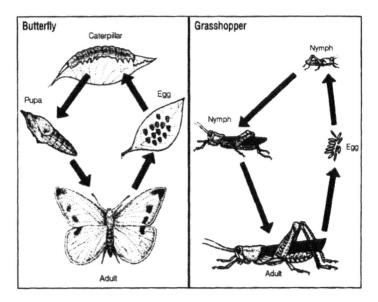

Let us look at metamorphosis in two insects.

The butterfly undergoes complete metamorphosis, that is, its life cycle runs into four stages: (a) egg (b) larva or caterpillar (c) pupa or chrysalis and (d) adult insect. The egg is usually laid on the undersurface of leaves. After a few days it hatches into a caterpillar which feeds on the leaves. This is the stage when the insect does greatest damage to the plant. When the caterpillar is fully grown, it stops feeding and falls to the ground. Here it enters into the pupal stage where a complete change of the body takes place. Soon the fully grown insect emerges, ready to start the cycle all over again.

Some insects may lack one or more of the stages that a butterfly undergoes and these are said to undergo incomplete metamorphosis. For example, the grasshopper lays an egg from which a nymph, that is, a baby grasshopper is hatched. The nymph undergoes several moultings until it becomes an adult insect.

Name one other insect which undergoes (a) complete metamorphosis and (b) incomplete metamorphosis.

Insects in agriculture

Insects are important in agriculture. Many of them are useful. Insects pollinate flowers which help to increase fruit production. Bees give honey and wax whilst the silkworm spins silk. Some insects are parasitic, that is, they feed on other insects that may be harmful to our crops.

The lady-bird beetle is a good example. It destroys and feeds on scale insects and plant lice.

Many insects are harmful. They destroy leaves, stems, flowers, fruits, tubers and even stored grains. They suck the juices of plants and are carriers of plant diseases. Aphids spread the bunchy top virus in pawpaw and the palm-weevil spreads the red-ring nematodes in coconuts.

Insects cause discomfort and injury to animals. The maggot fly deposits its maggots on cut and bruised surfaces of animals. These maggots bore and tunnel into the flesh of the animals. Lice suck blood and cause ulcers to the skin.

The pictures on pages 126 and 127 show you some types of damage done to our crops by insects.

The bee is a helpful insect

Insect control

Some insects bite, bore, or cut plants. Others suck the juices of plants and damage their tissues. Can you name two insects which bite and two which suck?

The kinds of damage done by insects depend upon their mouth parts and feeding habits. Mole crickets and grasshoppers have biting mouth parts, that is, jaws for biting and chewing. Aphids and scales have a proboscis which enables them to pierce and suck the juices of plants.

Insects are controlled in several ways. Here are a few methods in use.

Physical methods

a Hand-picking – caterpillars may be removed by hand and destroyed.

b Use of sticky papers – insects fly and rest on sticky papers. They get stuck tightly to the paper, cannot move and die.

c Insect traps – insects could be trapped and caught.

Use of insecticides

a Stomach poisons – biting insects such as mole crickets are induced to feed on poisoned baits. After a meal the insects die off. Do you know why the insects die?

b Contact poisons are very effective. They act on the nervous system of the insects from the time they get in contact with the insecticides.

Biological control

Some insect pests have natural enemies. For example, lady bird beetle and certain types of ants feed upon scale insects and aphids (plant lice). Where this occurs, the natural enemies of the insect pest should be encouraged and not destroyed.

Cultural methods

a Crop rotation

Do you remember what crop rotation means? It means the growing of different crops in succession on the same plot of land. Many insects attack and feed on a particular group or family of crops. By rotating crops these insects could be controlled.

b Sanitation

Garden plots and surroundings should be kept clean as they may harbour harmful insects. Old leaves and insect infested branches must be pruned and removed from cultivated plants.

c Selection of resistant varieties

Some crop varieties are hardy and more resistant than other varieties to certain types of insect attack. Where possible farmers should select resistant varieties for cultivation.

d Change of locality

The insect population which attacks a particular crop tends to increase and becomes difficult to control. When this happens, it is advisable to move and cultivate the crop in another locality where the insect pest may be absent.

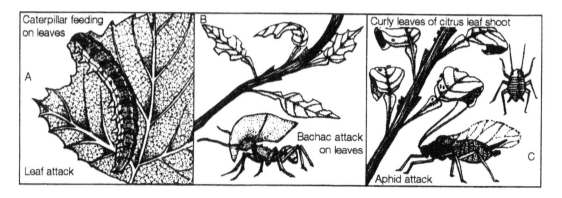

Caterpillar feeding on leaves

A

Leaf attack

B

Bachac attack on leaves

Curly leaves of citrus leaf shoot

Aphid attack

C

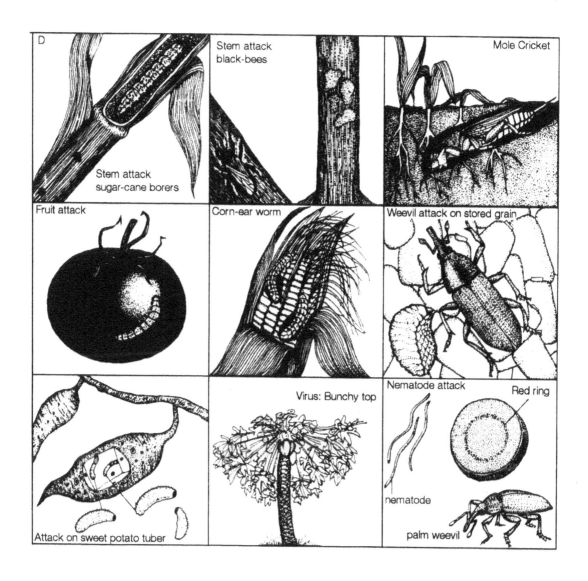

D

Stem attack
sugar-cane borers

Stem attack
black-bees

Mole Cricket

Fruit attack

Corn-ear worm

Weevil attack on stored grain

Attack on sweet potato tuber

Virus: Bunchy top

Nematode attack

Red ring

nematode

palm weevil

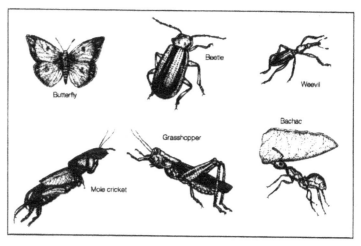

Butterfly

Beetle

Weevil

Mole cricket

Grasshopper

Bachac

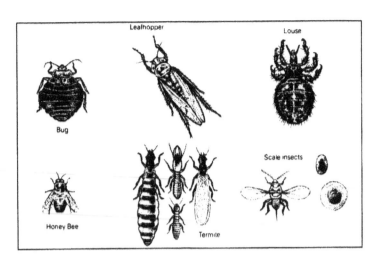

Integrated pest management

Many farmers put emphasis on the use of chemicals to control insect pests. They often ignore the physical, biological and cultural practices. The integrated pest management approach emphasises the practice of all the methods of insect pest control. The use of chemicals, however, should be the last resort, that is when the insect pest population becomes unmanageable and destructive.

Micro-organisms

What are micro-organisms? These are very tiny organisms which are not readily seen by the naked eye. They are best seen under a microscope. how does the microscope help you to see these organisms?

Fungi

Have you seen moulds growing on a slice of bread? These are fungi.
What is the colour of the fungi?
How do they obtain their nutrition?
How are they reproduced?
Fungi lack chlorophyll. They grow and feed on either living or dead matter or on both. They are reproduced by spores.

Some fungi like yeast and penicillium are useful. Others are responsible for decomposition and many of them cause diseases such as leaf and fruit spots, stem-rots, scabs and fusarium wilt as in tomatoes. Spraying with fungicides, controlled watering, and undercover cultivation are very helpful in controlling fungal diseases.

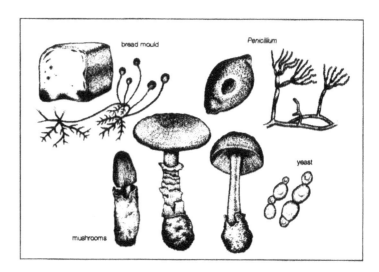

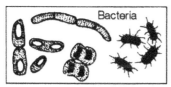

Bacteria

Bacteria are tiny organisms made up of single cells. They vary in size and shape and may live in little colonies.

Many bacteria are harmful to animals and plants as they cause diseases. Mastitis and tuberculosis in cattle are good examples of bacterial diseases in animals. Moko disease in banana and cabbage rot are both caused by bacteria. Crop rotation and sanitation practices are useful control measures for bacterial diseases in plants.

Some soil bacteria are very useful. They convert soil nitrogen into nitrates for plant use. Others capture atmospheric nitrogen and store it in root nodules. Root nodules are found in abundance in leguminous plants.

Nematodes

Nematodes are very minute worm-like organisms found in the soil. They attack and feed on the roots of plants. The wounds they cause expose the roots to further injury from fungi and bacteria. Some nematodes live inside the roots, forming knots in the root systems of the plants. The water channels in the roots are blocked and the plants suffer from a shortage of water and nutrient supplies. The use of nematicides and cultural practices are essential in the control of nematodes.

Root knot in lettuce

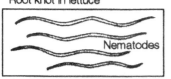

Other living creatures

The earthworm

The earthworm is a friend of the farmer. It thrives best in a damp clayey or loamy soil. It feeds on organic matter and

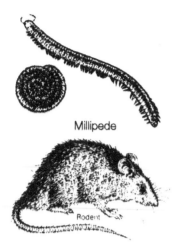

Millipede

Rodent

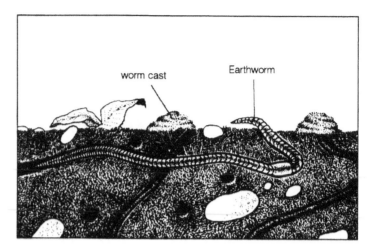

worm cast   Earthworm

soil which it passes out as a crumbly worm cast. This improves soil structure whilst the tunnels left in the soil help aeration and the movement of soil water.

Now try to find out how the animals in the pictures are useful or harmful in agriculture.

Summary

The biotic factors of the environment relate to living organisms. These include weeds, insects, soil micro-organisms and other living creatures.

Weeds are plants that are not wanted where they happen to be growing. They compete with cultivated plants for air, light, water and nutrient supplies. Weeds are controlled mechanically by weeding, brush cutting and ploughing or chemically by the use of herbicides.

Insects are found in almost every locality. Some of them like the honey bee and the silk worm are useful. Others like the mole cricket and aphids are harmful. They damage crops and animals by biting, sucking and boring. An insect is easily recognised by the structure of its body which is divided into three main parts (a) the head, (b) the chest and (c) the abdomen. In the early stages of their life-cycle they undergo metamorphosis which may be of the complete or incomplete type.

Insects are controlled in several ways. These include physical, chemical and biological methods as well as a variety of cultural practices. The emphasis, however, is on integrated pest management. This is an approach in which all the methods of control are used. Chemicals should be used as a last resort, and that is, only when the insect population becomes unmanageable and destructive.

Fungi, bacteria and nematodes are the main soil micro-organisms affecting plants. Fungi like yeast and penicillium are useful. Some others are responsible for decomposition and diseases in plants. Bacteria such as those causing mastitis, tuberculosis, moco disease and cabbage rot are harmful. However, those bacteria associated with legumes are useful. Some of them capture atmospheric nitrogen and store it in root nodules. Others convert soil nitrogen into nitrates.

Nematodes are minute worm-like organisms. Some of them live in the roots of plants causing blockage to water and nutrient absorption.

The use of fungicides, nematicides and good cultural practices are essential in controlling harmful soil micro-organisms.

Other living creatures affecting plants are earthworms, millipedes, rodents, birds, lizards and frogs. Most of these are friends of the farmer as they feed upon harmful insects and help in improving soil conditions. Rodents, like rats are harmful as they destroy chickens, garden crops and stored grains. They are controlled by poisoned baits and the use of traps.

Remember these

Biological control	The control of harmful insects or other organisms by means of their natural enemies.
Biting insect	An insect with jaws designed for cutting and chewing.
Chemical control	The use of chemicals to control pests and diseases.
Crop rotation	The growing of different crops in succession on the same plot of land. One of the crops is usually a legume.
Metamorphosis	The stages that an insect undergoes before it becomes an adult insect.
Resistant varieties	Those varieties showing immunity to attacks from certain pests and diseases.
Spiracles	Little opening or pores on the abdomen of an insect by means of which the insect breathes.
Sucking insect	An insect with mouth parts modified into a proboscis which is used for piercing and sucking.
Weeds	These are plants which happen to be growing where they are not wanted.
Worm cast	The digested organic matter and soil substances excreted by the earth worm on the surface of the ground.

Practical activities

1 Take a walk in your home or school garden and collect two different specimens of each of the following:
   a biting insects
   b sucking insects
   c soil macro-organisms
   d harmful weeds
   e insect pest attack
   Label the specimens indicating:
   a the name of the specimen
   b the date of collection
   c the place where the specimen was collected
   Your teacher will show you how to preserve these specimens.

2 Visit your school garden and collect specimens of soil found at the mouth or opening of:
   a an ant nest
   b the burrow of a lizard or rat
   Compare the two specimens looking specifically at the size and shape of the aggregates. Relate your observations to soil and soil improvement.

3 Observe a wasp or butterfly carefully. Make a drawing of the insect and label the body parts.

Do these test exercises

1 Consider these statements carefully. State whether they are *true* or *false*.

a All insects are harmful.

b Ploughing is a method of weed control.

c Biting insects have a proboscis.

d Earthworms thrive best in sandy soils.

e Red-ring disease in coconut is caused by a nematode.

2 Select the best answer from the choices given.

a An example of a soil micro-organism is:
A an earthworm
B a millipede
C a termite
D bacterium

b Identify the state in the life-cycle of an insect when it does greatest damage to plants.
A egg
B caterpillar
C pupa
D adult insect

c Which of these insects undergoes incomplete metamorphosis?
A mole cricket
B wasp
C pupa
D adult insect

d "Biological" control of insects refers to the control of insects by:
A an insecticide
B its natural enemies
C hand picking
D crop rotation practices

e Weeds compete with garden plants for:
(i) soil water and nutrient supplies
(ii) air and light
(iii) space on the garden plot
Of the statements above
A only (i) and (ii) are correct
B only (ii) and (iii) are correct
C only (i) and (iii) are correct
D (i), (ii) and (iii) are all correct

3 Complete the passage below by filling the blanks with words from this list:

subsoil, concerned, poisoned, burrowing, facilitate, sharp, damage, digging, traps, destroyed, farms.

Rats, rabbits and agouti are all rodents. They have .... teeth for gnawing and strong forelegs for .... When .... the ground they bring the .... to the surface. Their burrows .... air and water movement in the soil. Farmers are very .... about rats. They .... buildings, crops and chickens on the .... Rats could be .... by .... and .... baits.

4 a State two ways in which bacteria are useful to plants.
b List three harmful effects of nematodes on plants.
c Explain how the activities of earthworms improve soil conditions.

5 Say how these weeds are spread from one place to another:
amaranthus or bhaji, water grass, nutgrass, Bahama grass, Desmodium or sweetheart.

6 Fill in section B by selecting the correct answers from section C and associating them with Section A. The first is done for you.

A	B	C
– cuts leaves of plants	bachacs	nodules
– bore holes in fruits		flea-beetle
– cuts plants near to the ground		aphids
– bore holes in the leaves of plants		mole-cricket
– transmit nematodes that cause red-ring diseases		
– tunnels into building		butterfly
– shows incomplete metamorphosis		bachacs
– found in the roots of leguminous plants		palm weevil
– destroys plants in the caterpillar stage		termites
– transmits virus diseases		bees
		grasshopper

7 Write the general name for the chemicals that are used for destroying each of the following organisms. The first is done for you.

Organisms	Chemicals which destroy them
insects	insecticides
fungi	
nematodes	
bacteria	
weeds	

Appendix 1

Metric system

1 Some basic units

Physical quantity	Name	Symbol
Length	metre	m
Mass	kilogramme	kg
Time	second	s
Electric current	ampere	A
Temperature	degree celsius	°C

2 Some derived units

Physical quantity	Name	Symbol
Area	square metre	m^2
Volume	cubic metre	m^3
Speed	metre per second	m/s
Mass density	kilogramme per cubic metre	kg/m^3

3 Some common units of measure

a Fluid Measure
1,000 ml = 1 litre
1cc water = 1 ml = 1g
1 teaspoonful = 5cc

b Weight
1,000 g = 1 kilogramme
1,000 kg = 1 tonne

c Length
10 millimetres = 1 centimetre
100 centimetres = 1 metre
1,000 metres = 1 kilometre

d Area
1 square metre = 1 centare
100 square metres = 1 are
10,000 square metres = 1 hectare

e Temperature (degree celsius)
Freezing point = 0°C
Boiling point = 100°C
Body temperature (human) = 36.9°C

Normal rectal temperatures of certain animals (average)
chicken = 41.7°C
rabbit = 39.5°C
dog = 38.6°C
cat = 38.6°C
cow = 38.6°C
goat = 39.9°C
pig = 39.2°C

4 Incubation periods (average)
hens = 21 days
ducks = 29 days
geese = 29 days
turkeys = 29 days

5 Gestation periods (average)
rabbits = 31 – 32 days
goats = 150 – 152 days
pigs = 117 – 118 days
cows = 281 – 282 days

Appendix 2-Cropping guide table

Crop	Method of propagation	Best time to plant	Planting distances	General care and management	Crop ready for use
sweet potato	stem-cutting (40 cm long)	October	Ridges 75 cm apart. 38 cm apart on the ridges.	Plant slips on ridges. Turn vines on ridges periodically. Keep free from weeds. Spray with Sevin against leaf-eating insects. Harvest with fork avoiding damage to the tubers.	4–5 months
cassava	stem-cutting	May	1.3 m by 1.3 m	Soil well tilled and well drained. Keep free from weeds.	9–15 months
tannia	small corms	May–June	1 m by 60 cm	Plant in slight depressions filled with organic matter. Keep free from weeds. Earth up as the plant grows.	6–8 months
dasheen	corms	May–June	1 m by 60 cm	Dig holes or trenches 20 cm to 25 cm deep. Plant corms. Earth up as the plant grows. Keep plot free from weeds.	6–8 months
yam	tuber	April–May	Ridges 1 m apart 30 cm apart in the ridges.	Plant tubers not less than 112–140 g in weight. Dig trenches 40–45 cm deep and fill with organic matter. Pull earth to form ridges 30–40 cm high. Plant tubers in the ridges. Keep free from weeds and stake at vine formation.	
corn	seeds	May–June	Rows 1 m apart. 30 cm apart in the rows.	Soil well tilled and drained. Keep free from weeds. Need heavy applications of nitrogenous fertilisers, especially on poor soil types.	3–3 1/2 months
string beans	seeds	any time	25 cm by 25 cm	Till and drain plot. Work organic matter into the soil. Keep free from weeds and spray against fungal diseases.	6–7 weeks
bodi-beans (climber)	seeds	any time	Rows 60 cm apart. 75 cm between rows.	Till and drain soil properly. Incorporate pen-manure or organic matter into the soil. Keep plot free from weeds and stake at vine formation.	10–11 weeks
pigeon peas (tall type)	seeds	May–June	1.6 m by 1.6 m	Till, rotavate and drain soil properly. Add manure and organic matter in poor soils. Keep free from weeds.	8–9 months
cabbage	seeds	December May	Rows 60 cm apart. 45 cm in the rows.	Well tilled soil with a fine tilth. Ensure good drainage and incorporate organic matter into the soil. Sow seeds in seed boxes or seed beds. Apply nitrogenous fertilisers. Spray against caterpillar attack.	3 1/2–5 months

Crop	Method of propagation	Best time to plant	Planting distances	General care and management	Crop ready for use
cauliflower	seeds	any time	Rows 75 cm apart. 45 cm apart within the rows.	The same as for cabbage, except for the application of a mixed fertiliser just before flowering.	3 1/2–5 months
patchoi	seeds	any time	30 cm by 30 cm	Soil well drained and worked to a fine tilth. Sow seeds in seed-boxes or seed beds. Keep free from weeds. Apply nitrogenous fertilisers. Spray against caterpillar attack. Stop spraying two weeks before harvesting.	6–7 weeks
lettuce	seeds	any time	25 cm by 25 cm	Well drained soil worked to a fine tilth. Sow seeds in seed-boxes or seed beds. Transplant seedlings 5–6 weeks after sowing. Keep free from weeds. Apply nitrogenous fertilisers.	8–9 weeks
melongene	seeds	any time	1.3 m by 1.3 m	Soil well tilled and drained. Add pen-manure and organic matter into the soil. Apply nitrogenous fertilisers in the early stages followed by a 13.13.20 at flowering time. Keep free from weeds. Spray regularly against flea-beetle. Use an insecticide.	3–5 months
tomato	seeds	December–May	1 m by 60 cm	Till and drain soil. Add organic matter and work it well into the soil. Keep free from weeds. Spray against leaf miner and leaf boring insects. Moulding and staking may be very helpful.	3–3 1/2 months
sweet pepper	seeds	any time	75 cm by 60 cm	Till and drain soil. Incorporate organic matter. Sow seeds in seed boxes or seed beds. Transplant seedlings at 6 weeks old. Apply a 22.11.11 at transplanting and a 13.13.20 at flowering. Keep free from weeds.	2 1/2–3 months
cucumber	seeds	October–January	1.3 m by 1 m	Make gentle mounds using well rotted pen-manure. Sow seeds directly on mounds and thin out later on to three seedlings per stool. Keep free from weeds. Apply a 13.13.20 at flowering time.	7–8 weeks
pumpkins	seeds	October–February	2.6 m by 2.6 m	Prepare mounds as for cucumber. Sow seeds directly on plots and later on thin out to three seedlings per stool. Add 13.13.20 at flowering time. Keep free from weeds.	3 1/2–4 months

Crop	Method of propagation	Best time to plant	Planting distances	General care and management	Crop ready for use
carrots	seeds	any time	Drills 30 cm apart. 8 cm apart in drills.	Grows best on a loose fine sandy loam. Sow seeds in drill and thin out later on to 5–8 cm between plants in the drill. Gradually earth up as the plant grows up. After harvest, cut off tops and allow to dry before packaging.	3 months
ochroes	seeds	any time	60 cm by 75 cm	Work soil properly adding organic matter into it. Sow seeds directly into the ground and thin out to one or two plants per stool. Apply a 22.11.11 at planting time followed by a 13.13.20 at flowering time. Keep free from weeds. Spray against aphids.	8–10 weeks (harvest every 2–3 days)
sorrel	seeds	June–July	1.6 m by 1.6 m	Soil tilled and well-drained. Plant seeds 2 cm to 3 cm deep directly on the plots. Thin out after 3 weeks. Apply a mixed fertiliser (22.11.11) and follow up with a 10.10.20 (keep free from weeds).	6–7 months
celery	seeds	any time	25 cm by 25 cm	Sow seeds in seed boxes. Transplant 5 to 6 weeks later in well prepared plot with organic matter incorporated into the soil. Keep free from weeds. Apply nitrogenous fertilisers. Harvest leaves without damage to plants.	10–12 weeks
onions	seeds	November–December	Rows 25–30 cm apart and 8 cm apart in rows.	Till and drain soil. Apply organic matter and broadcast a supply of 10.15.10 into the soil. Keep free from weeds and give adequate supplies of water. Harvest when toppling of leaves about to occur. Leave to dry.	10–12 weeks
chives	(1) off-shoots or separates (2) seeds	May–November	22 cm by 22 cm	Prepare seeds in boxes. Transfer to garden plot at 10–15 cm in height. Mature chive clusters are separated, roots and tips pruned and then planted. Does well in a loamy soil rich in organic matter. Keep free from weeds.	3 1/2–4 months.

Index